COFFEE TABLE
PERSONAL
FINANCE

An Easy-to-Follow
Personal Finance Guide

Sterling Raskie, CFP®

About the author

Sterling Raskie is a fee-only financial planner at Blankenship Financial Planning in New Berlin, IL. He earned a PhD in financial and retirement planning from the American College of Financial Services. He is also a Senior Lecturer of Finance at the University of Illinois at Urbana-Champaign. He contributes to the blog *Getting Your Financial Ducks in A Row*, where he writes regularly about investments, retirement savings, and financial planning.

Sterling's research has been published in the *Journal of Financial Planning* and the *Journal of Financial Service Professionals*. His writing has appeared in MarketWatch, Forbes, Business Insider, USA Today, Wallet Hub, NAPFA Planning Perspectives, and The Motley Fool among others.

Sterling lives in Springfield, IL with his two daughters. In his spare time, he enjoys fly fishing, the outdoors, gardening, and time with his family.

Sterling welcomes any input or questions which can be emailed to him at: sterling.raskie@gmail.com.

Dedication

To my daughters Madeline and Delaney – thanks for your enduring, unconditional love and patience. I love you.

To my students – you humble me with your intelligence, drive, and curiosity.

To my clients – for allowing me to work with such wonderful, real people.

To my colleagues – for giving me the opportunity to surround myself with individuals much smarter than myself.

Acknowledgements

I want to acknowledge the efforts of my friends and colleagues who graciously helped this book become reality:

Larry Light, Jeff Stimpson, Jim Blankenship, CFP®, Robert Powell, Jessea Negless (Streetfire Design – cover), Geoff and Jamie Briggs (Vahalla Hills Farm, LLC), Jeffrey R. Brown, PhD.

I am grateful for your insight and expertise.

Disclaimer

It is not the intent of this publication or its author to provide professional tax, investment, or legal advice.

The strategies contained herein may not be suitable for your situation. You should consult with a professional where appropriate.

This book should only be used as a general guide.

Table of Contents

Introduction

If you're reading this book, chances are you're considering or have perhaps begun your wealth management journey. It's not uncommon to feel overwhelmed, intimidated, and generally flummoxed as to where to begin.

This book can be a starting point. It won't be a cure-all but will at least get you going in the right direction. As your situation changes, I recommend you seek additional help, advice, and professional opinions from qualified, competent professionals as needed.

A friend once asked me, "What's the biggest obstacle people face in financial planning?" My reply was sticking to their plan. The concepts presented in this book are not inherently difficult. They just need to be *done*.

Get started. Take action. Stick to your plan. Reflect. Revise.

Finally, should you have questions, please feel free to contact me at sterling.raskie@gmail.com.

Good luck!

Just Getting Started

At a point in some people's lives, they conclude they need some sort of assistance with their financial situation. This could be a recent high school or college grad determined to start off on the right track, or those in their mid to late careers wondering if what they're doing is the "right" way of doing things financially. In either case, the hope may be to make as few mistakes as possible along the way.

When considering this situation, there are a few things to look at first, before moving on to other planning areas. In other words, think of the following as a good foundation to have before expanding on or continuing your wealth management plan. This is the direction this book will take.

- Emergency Fund. This is the money set aside to pay for non-discretionary expenses that will not go away in the event of an emergency (loss of a job, medical, etc.). Although the amount and time frame for the emergency fund may vary, a good rule of thumb is to set aside at least three to six months of non-discretionary expenses. Some individuals may choose to go to nine months or even a year.

This protects individuals so they do not have to leverage expenses on a credit card, home equity, or dig into precious retirement or college savings. As non-discretionary expenses increase, so should the emergency fund.

However, non-discretionary expenses don't have to increase arbitrarily. Be cognizant of whether an increase makes sense (e.g. higher rent, mortgage, car payment, etc.). Which leads to the next point.

- Levels of Debt. Look at all the debt that is outstanding. Mortgage, car payments, credit card, student loans, and other debt. If there's none – congratulations! If there is, consider the impact the debt has on retirement savings, college savings, and other wealth building assets. Debt payments could be replaced with cash flows to these assets to build wealth.

  Arguably, the only debts worth having are a home loan (leveraging an asset) or student loans (investing in human capital) – but even these debts should be paid off as quick as possible.

Being over-leveraged makes or causes delays or shortages to retirement and college funding. It makes us susceptible to working just to pay current debts, instead of working to fund long-term goals.

- Risk Management. Before building wealth, it must be preemptively protected, then proactively protected. This is where insurance plays a less-glamourous, but critical role.

  Life insurance protects human capital (current and future wages) from pre-mature death, disability insurance protects income if we can no longer work due to disability. Auto insurance protects us against liability from auto accidents and homeowner's insurance provides liability protection in addition to protecting (for many individuals) our largest asset. An umbrella policy (which everyone should have) provides additionally liability should limits be exceeded on underlying policies.

  Health insurance covers illness so we do not become insolvent if we get sick, while long-term care insurance may be necessary to preserve wealth due to long-term care needs. Annuities (the other life insurance) may be necessary to protect against outliving one's income.

While not exhaustive, these are the general areas to think about then first getting started or continuing with your wealth management plan.

Baby Steps

One of my favorite movies is be *What About Bob?* starring Richard Dreyfus and Bill Murray. Fans of the film will remember Bob Wiley, a neurotic, compulsive individual who seeks out the advice and care of Dr. Leo Marvin. The title of Dr. Marvin's book that he gives to Bob is called *Baby Steps* – the idea that anything is manageable and possible if you take baby steps.

Baby steps are important in our everyday life. Whether it be pursuing a degree, saving for retirement, or even trying to change or break a habit – you need to take it one step at a time to achieve the goal. And sometimes, *just moving forward,* even at a snail's pace is progress.

Take saving money for example. Some people may think it's tough to save, especially if their budget is already tight. These people can try baby steps. Even starting out very modestly at a dollar a month adds up to $12 per year saved. Granted we're not looking at buying a second home in retirement with this, but it's $12 saved they otherwise wouldn't have.

Need to get up earlier in the day? Try setting your alarm one minute early each day for 30 days. By taking baby steps you'll have an extra 30 minutes at the end of a month. How about starting to exercise? Try walking around the block for a few weeks, then gradually try jogging around the block. Then, the next couple of blocks and soon you're running a mile – nonstop.

I think you get the point – start small, but start. If you have an IRA or a 401(k), start saving 1% per paycheck – then gradually increase that over time. Have a bad habit of spending money on lunch and coffee every day? Start small – pack a lunch and bring a thermos one day a week. If you like the extra money in your pocket, you can choose to do it more regularly.

By taking baby steps toward your goals you'll be able to look back at the leap you've made from where you first began.

Chapter 0 – First Things First

Check Your Vitals

When you go to the doctor for a check-up what's the first thing he or she usually does? The doctor checks your vitals. Generally, this is heartrate, blood pressure, breathing, reflexes, etc. Sometimes the doctor will have a questionnaire asking various questions such as number of drinks per day, whether you smoke, and any allergies – to name a few.

Most individuals give this information without thinking twice. Most of the time, the answers we give don't change. So why does the doctor keep asking the same questions every time we have an appointment? The answer is because if one of these answers does change (such as an irregular heartbeat or high blood pressure) this changes the potential diagnoses and outcome.

For your personal finances, it's also important to check your vitals. In other words, even though you think you're financially fit, continue to review your auto, home, life, health, and disability insurance to check coverage and liability limits. Most of the time an individual is going to be ok.

However, there are times where someone thinks they're fine, yet their coverage is inadequate. For example, maybe the individual has comprehensive and collision deductibles on vehicles that are old. The coverage was necessary 10 or 15 years ago, but not today. This would be the equivalent of being on antibiotics for an illness, but still taking them when the illness is cured – and continuing to pay for the prescription!

Additionally, levels of debt and savings should be checked frequently. Are debt ratios improving or getting worse? Has your savings rate changed or does it need to be changed? Someone saving $50 per paycheck when starting a job may need to increase that amount as they receive salary increases. If left unchecked, someone can wind up with considerably less in retirement, yet their earnings allowed them to save more.

Your financial vitals should be checked at least annually, or every time individuals meet with their financial professionals. Most of the time things don't change dramatically. But if they do, you can be better prepared to move forward with an accurate diagnosis of the situation and the appropriate prescription to remedy the issue.

Creating an Emergency Fund

Putting away some money for sudden expenses is a good idea. But how much? Here's how to figure that out.

This is money set aside for a rainy day. If you are faced with unexpected expenses from a car accident, disability, storm damage to your home, losing a job, an ill family member or theft, your savings could take a big hit without an emergency fund in place.

Generally, a good place to start is a goal of at least three to six months of non-discretionary living expenses.

These are expenses that do not go away when you lose your job or the ability to generate income. Included are your mortgage payment or rent, utilities, food, car payment and taxes.

Now comes the easy part. Simply add up all of your non-discretionary living expenses that you have in a month and multiply by three or six. This is the amount you need to set aside. For example, if you have a $1,200 mortgage, eat $400 in groceries per month and pay $300 for utilities, you have a total of $1,900 in monthly expenses. So your emergency fund needs to be between $5,700 and $11,400.

Of course, this is just a rule of thumb that doesn't apply to everyone. The amount you need also depends on your job, income and how you're paid. A tenured college professor making $6,500 monthly, only needs a few months' expenses put away.

The head of a large company earning $20,000 monthly or a commissioned sales person making $10,000 monthly should have nine to 12 months stashed away. This is because there's a good chance of not finding another job at that income level if you are fired or laid off. And generally, as peoples' incomes increase, so do their expenses.

Saving the money is not that hard. It just takes a bit of planning and discipline. You can start by putting away a small sum every week or month, depending on what works for you. This could be as little as $50 per month until you funded the account.

If you're looking for places to find money, cut unnecessary expenses until your emergency fund is at 100%. Reduce your phone bill, cut your cable TV costs and pack your lunch instead of dining out. Notice a pattern? These are all discretionary expenses that can go away if you want them to. You can also use your emergency fund in tandem with your insurance deductibles. Let's say you have low deductibles on your auto insurance and want to save some money. You can simply increase your deductibles, which lowers your insurance premiums. If you need to use your deductible for a claim, you can take from your emergency fund.

This is wise especially if you rarely file claims. Should you have a disability policy with 60 days before benefits start, your emergency fund can help cover expenses in the meantime.

An emergency fund is not a slush fund to buy toys like a new car or TV. It's not money to play with, gamble with or dip into. Don't steal from yourself. Resist the temptation to spend it. If you feel uncontrollably tempted, put the money in an account that's not easy to get to. Example: a money market account where you limit checks to a certain amount, like $250. This curbs the urge to spend on little things.

Where you save this money is important too. Put it away in a relatively liquid instrument such as a savings, checking or money market account. This is important because other accounts such as certificates of deposit or retirement savings accounts charge heavy fees for early withdrawals. Retirement accounts should stay as such. A properly funded emergency fund eliminates the need to rely on premature retirement account distributions when you need cash.

Where to Keep Emergency Funds

The ideal size of your fund depends on such factors as the number of incomes in your household, your earnings from such other sources as pensions or investments, your access to a home equity line of credit and your overall cost of living. Many people also underestimate expenses or only consider fixed expenses such as a mortgage or car payments. Examine your *whole* budget.

With the disappearance of savings accounts paying much more than miserly interest (if any at all), one big question becomes where to invest your emergency fund. Your fund needs to be liquid; you need easy access to the money without having to wait days, weeks or months.

One suggestion: Put your emergency fund in a checking or savings account. Though the Federal Deposit Insurance Corp. (FDIC) insures you up to $250,000, don't expect to earn big interest; a general savings or checking account pays very little interest.

Your other major choice is a money market account from a bank, discount brokerage house or other financial institution. These accounts are liquid and stable – usually invested in bonds and other low-yielding securities. As seems a trend among such assets these days, money markets also pay little interest, usually around 1% or less.

The point is not high rates of return, which generally means more exposure to risk. Don't risk your emergency fund *at all*.

For example, putting your disaster money in an aggressive stock mutual fund (which I don't recommend) may get you better returns. Your safety net for a dire situation can also shrivel – even vanish – in a market crash or correction. You can be left with a fraction of the money you originally used to fund the account.

That's bad news indeed in a financial emergency.

Chapter 1 – Risk Management

Auto Insurance Explained

Most individuals who drive a vehicle have that vehicle insured (or should). In many states (including Illinois) auto insurance is mandatory. However, mandatory does not mean adequate. Even the phrase "full coverage" does not indicate adequate coverage for a person or family. The following is a breakdown of what coverages are generally provided on an auto policy, and some ideas regarding the amount those coverages should be.

A. Liability. This coverage is for you or a permitted driver of your vehicle that provides liability coverage in the event you are liable for bodily injury from an auto accident. This coverage provides bodily injury protection on a per person and per accident basis. There's also coverage for property damage.

Coverages are stated in thousands of dollars. For example, 250/500/100 means $250,000 of bodily injury protection per person, $500,000 total per accident, and $100,000 property damage coverage. Coverage amounts can be higher (or lower), but 250/500/100 is the minimum one should have.

B. Medical Payments. This coverage is provided to you and occupants of your vehicle for injuries sustained or for you if you're struck by a vehicle while as a pedestrian (e.g. walking in a crosswalk and hit by a car). Coverage is usually from $1,000 to $5,000 per person, per occurrence.

C. Uninsured/Under-Insured Motorist. This coverage provides you and occupants of your vehicle coverage in the event another party is liable for your injuries and doesn't have enough of their own insurance coverage (liability) to cover your injuries or they don't have any insurance at all. Generally, these amounts are going to be identical to Coverage A amounts on your policy.

D. Coverage for Damage to Your Vehicle (Comprehensive and Collision). This coverage is what most people think of when they hear "full coverage". Full coverage meaning there's the required liability protection (Coverage A) along with the optional Coverage D (comp and collision). Let's break comp and collision down further.

   a. Comprehensive (or sometimes called Other Than Collision) is coverage for damage to your vehicle arising from theft, vandalism, colliding with a bird, deer, or other animal, glass damage, fire, hail. Generally, there a deductible involved (your sharing in the loss). After the deductible is met, then insurance pays the remainder for damages. Generally, the higher the deductible, the lower the premium. In many cases, damage from comprehensive losses are not considered at-fault (they won't increase your premiums).

   b. Collision is coverage for damage to your vehicle arising from hitting another car, running off the road, hitting a tree, driving into a lake. Like comprehensive, there will be a deductible involved after which the insurance company will pay for the damages. Unlike comprehensive, in most cases a collision claim will result in an at-fault accident that will likely raise your premiums.

c. For both comp and collision consider the age of the vehicle and the age of the driver. If the vehicle is older (10+ years) consider dropping these coverages and carrying liability only. If you have a young (teen) driver, consider rating he or she on a vehicle with liability only. Naturally, you may not have the choice if you have a lien on the vehicle. In that case, the lender may require comp and collision with specific deductibles.

Here are some other aspects of auto insurance that are good to know. In most cases, your coverage will extend to rental vehicles (check with your carrier to be sure). This means many individuals can skip the extra insurance pitched to them when renting a car while on business or vacation.

Insurance follows the vehicle. This means that if you borrow someone's car or they borrow yours and there's an accident, the insurance used first is the insurance that is on the vehicle involved in the accident, regardless of driver.

Additionally, most policies will not provide coverage outside of the US. Some exceptions are Canada and within a certain distance inside the border of Mexico. Again, check with your specific carrier.

Finally, many carriers will specifically exclude coverage for auto racing, driving a vehicle without permission, business use, being an Uber or Lyft driver, or regular use of a vehicle by a driver not underwritten on the policy.

Homeowner's Insurance Explained

If you're a homeowner or contemplating home ownership, chances are you've thought about home insurance. For many individuals, their home is their largest asset. It's also an asset generally acquired with leverage – that is, you usually borrow money to buy your home and have a mortgage for 15 or 30 years.

As one of your biggest assets, it's important to protect your home with homeowner's insurance. Homeowner's insurance provides coverage for your home in the event it's damaged by a peril such as a fire, tornado, etc.

Additionally, your home policy provides coverage for incidents you may be liable for – such as someone injured on your property due to your negligence.

Your home insurance policy is broken down in the following ways.

   A. Dwelling coverage. This is the maximum coverage your policy provides for damage to your home. For example, a home with dwelling coverage of $250,000 would have coverage for damages or loss to the home up to $250,000. Often, the price you paid for your home will not line up with the coverage from your insurance carrier. This is normal. Your home is being insured for what it would take to rebuild it, not what it sold for. Your home should be insured for at least 80% of its replacement value (more on this in the next section).

B. Separate structures. Separate structures coverage provides coverage for buildings and structures detached from your home – the most common being a detached garage. Sheds may also be included. Generally, separate structures coverage is 10% of the dwelling amount. If the dwelling is insured for $250,000, separate structures are covered for $25,000. More coverage can be purchased if needed.

C. Personal Property. Personal property coverage provides coverage for all your stuff. This includes furniture, appliances, clothes, TVs, computers, etc. Coverage for personal property is usually 50% of the dwelling amount. Keeping with our same example, a home insured for $250,000 would have personal property coverage at $125,000, with more available to purchase if necessary.

D. Loss of Use. Loss of use provides coverage in the event you have to vacate your home due to damages while it's being repaired. For example, if your home is damaged from a fire and you must stay in a hotel for a few weeks while your home is being repaired, loss of use coverage will help cover the expense of the hotel stay.

E. Liability. Arguably the most important coverage on your home policy is the one least often thought about – liability. Liability provides coverage in the event you're legally liable (negligent) for someone's injuries while on your premises. Examples may include someone slipping on your icy driveway, a child injured on your backyard trampoline, a pool accident.

If you're found liable for someone's injuries or death, the likelihood of a lawsuit is high. Liability coverage will provide coverage for the injured person's medical bills, and your legal defense. Liability coverage should be at least $500,000 but can be higher if wanted.

F. Medical Payments to Others. Medical payments to others provides coverage in the event someone (not living in the household) is injured at your home. For example, someone trips while walking down your stairs and injures themselves. You're not at fault, and you're not admitting fault, however this coverage can provide for their medical expenses. Notice that the terminology is medical payments to *others* – which means it only covers individuals not in your household.

The type of home you have will dictate which coverage you need. Whether you're a homeowner, renter, condo owner, etc., will determine the type of policy you need. An experienced insurance professional can provide guidance regarding the type of policy that's best for you.

Lastly, once your policy is in place, consider reviewing it annually for any changes, or updates (home improvements are common), to your home.

Renter's Insurance

If you're considering living in an apartment or currently reside in one, it's important to make sure you have renter's insurance. Renter's insurance is an often-overlooked risk management tool for an overall financial plan, but it's critical for protecting your assets and liability.

Renter's insurance covers your personal property in your apartment. This includes clothes, furniture, electronics – pretty much all your stuff. It also provides liability coverage. This means that if you're liable for damages to the apartment complex, someone's injured in your apartment, or you're liable for other damages, the liability coverage provides an amount to help pay for these damages. In other words, if you're found liable or negligent it doesn't come out of your pocket. The renter's insurance pay for it.

A typical renter's insurance policy can provide $15,000 of protection for your personal property (you can get more if needed) and $100,000 for liability coverage. However, consider $300,000 of liability coverage or higher, just to be safe. You may also consider an umbrella policy to provide liability coverage above and beyond your renter's policy (for catastrophic losses).

The cost for renter's insurance is relatively cheap. You can expect to pay about $150-$200 in annual premiums. This could differ depending on your location, personal property, etc. Bundling your renter's policy with your auto insurance with the same company may also save you money with a multi-policy discount.

So, if you're considering or currently renting an apartment, consider getting a renter's insurance policy or reviewing your current policy for updates. For a small amount of money per year it will provide thousands of dollars in coverage.

The Power of Endorsements

Many homeowner's policies do not cover or provide very limited coverage on specific items such as jewelry, antiques, coins, firearms, etc. Generally, if there is coverage for these items it's for an aggregate amount not to exceed a certain dollar limit – such as $1,000 for the *total* amount lost.

For example, Herb has an extensive coin collection worth $50,000 and his wife Peaches has an engagement ring worth $10,000. Under their normal home policy, if there was a theft, fire, or tornado causing a total loss of their coins and ring, they may only get up $2,000 (assuming the aggregate coverage amount was $1,000 respectively). This puts them at a $58,000 loss.

Both Peaches and Herb could have prevented this by adding an endorsement to their homeowner's policy. Think of an endorsement as an "insurance policy within the main policy". An endorsement specifically covers an article of personal property that is either excluded or not fully covered in the main policy.

With an endorsement, the owner can choose their own deductible for the loss and coverage is much more inclusive. This means that if the homeowner's policy deductible is $500, the endorsement can have a deductible for, say, Peaches' ring for $100. In this case, their loss would only be the deductible on the endorsement – a considerably smaller sum.

Additionally, many endorsements will cover mysterious disappearance. This means that should Peaches lose her ring washing dishes, it's likely covered with the endorsement, something the homeowner's policy wouldn't. Also, an endorsement supersedes any conflicting terminology in the main policy.

Endorsements are an inexpensive way to broaden coverage under an existing policy. Should you have an extensive collection or an item of considerable value, an endorsement may be worth considering.

Umbrella Policies: A Good Deal

Is a personal liability umbrella policy worth the price? Generally, yes. The price remains reasonable even as the expense of just minor accidents continues to skyrocket.

Personal liability umbrella policies cover above and beyond the underlying liability limits on your auto or homeowner's insurance. You can also buy umbrella policies if you hold renter's insurance or condo policies.

According to the carrier Geico, umbrella insurance covers bodily injuries (medical bills and liability claims resulting from injuries due to an auto accident that's your fault, for example) and property damage (such as to vehicles and other property that are your fault). You're also covered if sued for slander or libel or false arrest, among other personal liabilities.

Umbrella liability usually comes in increments of $1 million. Most people buy the coverage through their carrier for auto or home insurance. That carrier usually requires that in an underlying auto policy the personal liability of the policy be at least a specific amount, often $250,000 or higher.

Likewise with a home policy: The insurer requires the liability reach at least a certain amount, often $300,000 or higher.

The umbrella policy pays after accidents and liability exhaust the above amounts. If you're liable for an auto accident or an accident at your home (trampoline injuries and pool mishaps are common), the insurance company pays from your auto or home policy first; damages left over then come from your umbrella policy.

For example, suppose driver Danny crosses the center line and hits another car head-on. All three passengers in the other car sustain serious injuries totaling $750,000 in liability. Danny's auto policy pays $250,000 of bodily injury per person and $500,000 total per accident.

Danny's policy covers $500,000 of the damages and then runs out. If Danny lacks umbrella coverage, he pays the remaining $250,000 and might suffer wage garnishment or seizure of assets, among other drawn-out collection scenarios that make for a bad life.

Luckily, Danny carries $1 million in umbrella coverage, which takes care of the remaining $250,000 – including any legal defense. Umbrella coverage makes sure he has just a bad day.

Umbrella policies may also cover your liability even if an accident didn't occur under circumstances that engage your auto or home policies. Typically, umbrella policies pay after you pay a self-insured retention (deductible) of some $1,000 to $5,000.

Prices for umbrella coverage are reasonable and fluctuate based on such factors as risk exposure. For example, a single person with one car, one home and no moving violations or at-fault accidents pays about $150 to $200 in premiums *annually*. A couple with two cars, a home, a boat, all-terrain vehicles and teenage drivers pays much more because of the increased risk, maybe $500 to $750 annually.

Why so cheap? The underlying insurance requirement on umbrella policies must be high; rarely do claims exceed these amounts and trigger umbrella benefits. Insurance companies know the low percentage of umbrella policies that pay and that these policies are, for them, cash cows.

Is umbrella coverage a good idea? Yes. If the worst happens, do you want a bad day or a bad life?

Life Insurance: Protect Your Most Important Asset

You may think that your most important asset is your home, your nest egg, your priceless collection of Etruscan snoods. Your most important asset is you – your human capital. Your human capital is your current and future economic contributions to your family.

Perhaps you've gone to college and majored in a profession to pursue a career. You may have earned advanced degrees and designations to increase your knowledge, professionalism, and income.

All of this increases your human capital – your ability to earn, substantially, over your lifetime.

Now that you have a family, a spouse and kids to support, you need to hedge your human capital, you need to protect it in the event it's lost – should you die unexpectedly.

No one likes talking about death. Even writing these words, it's hard to type them. But it's necessary to convey the importance of life insurance.

Life insurance protects your human capital, the income you receive because of your human capital, and the support your human capital provides for your family.

Without life insurance, should you die, so does the financial support you're providing to your family. In other words, life insurance isn't for you, it's for those you leave behind.

Having enough life insurance means your survivors, your family being able to continue paying the mortgage, bills, tuition, buying groceries, and continue saving for retirement and or college educations. It also allows them enough time to grieve without having to worry about financial obligations.

So how much life insurance should you have? A general rule of thumb is approximately 10 to 16 times your gross income. Of course, this is a *basic* guideline. You may need more depending on your circumstances – such as your age. You typically need more when you're young versus when you're older. This is because when you're young, you have a lot longer earnings time horizon that needs to be protected. This generally decreases as you age.

In the next section, we'll cover the different types of life insurance policies available and which one(s) is most likely your best choice.

What is the Best Life Policy to Buy?

When researching the appropriate life insurance to buy you're faced with a myriad of choices. Term, whole life, universal life, variable universal life are just a few of the policies that may be presented, if not *sold*, to you.

Which policy is best? It depends.

If someone is looking for the best bang for their buck and wants to purchase the most insurance for the least amount of money, term is going to be your best bet. Term is cheap, builds no cash value, and is used if you have a time frame where you need insurance – such as a 30-year term for a 30-year mortgage or 30-year term until your retirement).

When you purchase term, know that it will run out – which is why it's called term. It lasts for a specific term and then ends. When the term insurance expires, you may then "self-insure" at death in retirement since you'll have saved enough in assets that if you die, your spouse can live off the financial assets accumulated. Proponents of term will buy term and invest the difference of what the premium would have been for a permanent policy such as whole life.

Whole life insurance is a permanent product and is generally more expensive than term. For the premium you pay you'll get permanent coverage for life and the policy will build some cash value as you age and keep paying premiums.

Whole life will typically pay either a guaranteed interest rate (maybe 2-4%) or dividends based on the insurance company's investment experience. Proponents (sellers) of whole life will argue that it's a forced way to save money and will argue proponents of buy term and invest the difference rarely do.

Polices like universal life and variable universal life offer premium flexibility which say a policyholder can vary the amount of premiums paid any given month. Variable universal life, or VUL, will also let the policy owner direct the investments or cash value of the policy in different subaccounts that invest in stock and bond mutual funds. In a VUL, the cash value can fluctuate, and interest is not guaranteed as it will rise and fall according to how the underlying investments do.

So which policy is best? Admittedly, I am biased toward term. As a financial planner I believe in the buy term and invest the difference philosophy. After all, shouldn't a good planner know where to invest the rest and help the client save the difference? I will also admit that I own whole life – not on me – but on my children. This is to protect their insurability. Should any of them ever fall ill and become uninsurable in the future, they'll always have their whole life policies.

But, caveat emptor – buyer beware. Several permanent policies have long, hefty surrender charges. This means that for the first 7 to 15 years of the policy if you surrender it or cancel it, you'll get less than 100% of your cash value.

In addition, permanent policies typically pay much higher commissions – so advisors who sell permanent life insurance may be biased to sell you the permanent policy. Commissions can be as high as 50% of the annual premium for permanent policies and about 40% for term. Since term is cheaper, less commissions are paid.

And – life insurance is NEVER an investment. Any advisor who says differently is *selling* you something. Life insurance is just that – life insurance.

In the end, the life insurance decision should be yours, with any advice given to you by an objective advisor or agent. Don't be afraid to ask how much commission they'll make off the product and why they're recommending the product they're selling. If the advisor or agent is captive (they work for a parent company) ask if they can only offer their company's policies. This should be disclosed.

Finally, shop around. You may find a good deal online or you may find a good deal asking your current auto and home agent if they offer life insurance. Often companies will offer discounts on all three policies if you keep all your insurance business under one roof.

Buy Term and Invest the Difference?

A topic often argued in the financial service world is whether an individual should buy term and invest the difference or buy a cash value life insurance policy.

On one side you'll have someone arguing that an individual should buy a cash value life insurance policy. This individual (maybe a salesperson) will argue that buying a cash value life insurance policy (e.g. whole life) is a better option for a client since it generates cash value over time and "forces" the client to save. Often, they'll argue that the client wouldn't save for retirement or college otherwise.

The flip side of that argument suggests the client should buy term life insurance and invest the difference in price from the whole life policy and the term life policy in a qualified savings plan such as a Roth IRA. Before we look at some numbers let's look at how whole life and Roth IRAs work. We can compare these two vehicles as both are considered to have tax-free growth, tax-free withdrawals (generally), and pass tax-free to heirs at death.

Whole life policies are life insurance policies with a cash savings component. Generally, premiums are level and fixed throughout the policy duration –

which is to usually to age 100 or 120. In the early years of the policy more of the premium paid funds the cash value account (since the cost of insurance is low) and in the later years less goes to the cash account and more premium is used to fund the cost of insurance.

If premiums are paid, the coverage lasts the client's entire life. Should the client live to age 100 or age 120, the policy endows, and the client will receive the entire death benefit, consisting entirely of their own cash value. Should an individual need or want cash from the policy, they are allowed tax-free loans or withdrawals. Death benefits are passed to beneficiaries tax-free.

Roth IRAs allow an individual to save up to $6,500 ($7,000 if age 50 or older) annually. After-tax money goes into the Roth and the money grows tax deferred and qualified distributions are tax-free. The Roth IRA also passes to the beneficiary tax-free.

A key difference between the two products is access to funds. For example, if the client wanted to cancel or surrender the whole life policy in the early policy years, they would incur a surrender charge and forfeit a percentage of the cash value. Surrender periods can last up to 15 years.

Roth IRAs allow access to the *principal* at any time without penalty. This is because the principal has already been taxed. Earnings may be subject to taxes and penalties, depending on the client's age. Another big difference is one vehicle is life insurance and the other is a tax-qualified retirement plan. They should be kept separate.

Using quote information from a nationally known insurer we gather two quotes; one 30-year term and one whole life. The term quote was for a 35-year-old male as was the whole life quote. The 30-year term premium was $80 monthly and the whole life premium was $660 monthly. The face amount for both was $500,000.

The difference between the two policies is $580. Of course, our 35-year-old male cannot exceed $6,500 annually ($500 monthly) to his Roth IRA so we use the monthly contribution of $500. This still leaves over $80 for him to save or invest elsewhere (maybe a 529 for his kids?). The term is $960 annually and the whole life policy is $7,920! Remember, the salesperson makes about 50% commission on each policy.

For the Roth IRA let's assume a 5 percent rate of return over a 30-year time horizon. We also do not assume any indexed contribution increases. In 30 years the client has $416,129 in his Roth. Arguably this would be more considering indexed increases. However, this is a bit less than the $500,000 death benefit in the whole life policy should the client pass away.

The 30-year term has now expired. With a whole-life policy, the client is still paying $660 monthly. However, less premium dollars are funding the cash account, and more are funding the cost of insurance. We would argue that at this age, the client could reasonably "self-insure". That is, use funds from the Roth to fund burial and final expenses; a strategy planned and used by many term insurance holders. In addition, they don't have the monthly expense of life insurance premiums from a whole life policy throughout retirement.

Let's assume that the client retires right at 65 and no longer makes any Roth contributions. Withdrawals are now tax-free from the Roth. Let's also assume that the client decides to not take any withdrawals. If the money in the Roth at age 65 simply sits and continues to earn 5 percent over the next 35 years (until the client is age 100) the Roth grows to $2,295,376 or $1,795,000 more than what he'd receive from the whole life policy.

Should the client die right at age 100 his heirs receive the amount tax-free, just like they would in the life policy. And, earnings in the inherited Roth continue to grow tax-free. Life insurance death benefits, while initially tax-free, receive no tax-free benefits on the growth of the original death benefit.

Let's look at another option. Let's assume the client has access to a Roth 401(k). Now he can save the entire $580 per month. Using our new monthly contribution to the Roth 401(k) he has saved $482,710 by age 65. If he lets it sit until age 100 (we assume he rolls over to a Roth IRA before age 70 to avoid RMDs) his amount at age 100 is $2,662,635.

This is pretty strong evidence that buying term and investing the difference does make sense for most individuals.

There are instances where permanent life insurance may be a viable option for cash savings and additional retirement funding. High net worth and ultra-high net worth individuals may benefit from cash value life insurance as part of their wealth management plan. If this is you, talk to a professional (discussed later), as the discussion is beyond the scope of this book.

Do I Need My Life Insurance Through Work?

Generally, life coverage from an employer is group term coverage paying a death benefit up to a certain amount, usually based on a multiple of your salary. If you make $50,000 per year, for instance, your group term insurance pays a death benefit of $50,000.

(Once a term policy expires, you decide whether to renew it or to let the coverage end. In addition to being cheaper than whole life or other life insurance types, term offers protection against of number of different bad scenarios and sells for several different spans of time.)

Your employer often pays the premium for coverage up to a certain death benefit (usually $50,000). Why? The Internal Revenue Service allows your employer to pay the premiums on a group life insurance policy up to that amount because the IRS figures anything above it counts as taxable compensation to you the employee.

Sometimes you can elect coverage for a higher benefit amount but probably must pay for the extra coverage out of your own pocket. Best to shop around, of course, for the best term rates.

As an example, your employer may pay the premiums for the first $50,000 in death benefit but allows you to elect up to five times your salary for group term coverage. If you take that option, you have a $250,000 death benefit but *you* pay the premium for the additional $200,000 in coverage.

We all hear about the golden goodies like subsidized health insurance and employer matches of retirement funds. Is employer-sponsored life insurance also a good deal? You bet.

Often this is the most insurance you can get with almost no underwriting involved. This means even with poor health or a pre-existing condition, you may get life insurance coverage at a reasonable price. Buy the most group term life insurance you can and supplement any additional term insurance need with coverage from a reputable insurance company.

Although group life can be a cost-effective way to get life insurance, your premiums may change as you age. In other words, your group coverage may be more expensive than a similar private policy as you get older. In this case, assuming you can get insurance outside of work, it may make more sense to compare premiums between your employer policy and a private policy and go with the cheaper policy.

Some employer policies are portable; you can take the coverage with you if you leave your employer. You usually do this via what's called conversion: The group term policy converts to an individual permanent policy such as whole life or universal life.

Though you can convert without going through underwriting, the premiums are likely sky-high. This makes the most sense if it's the only insurance you can get and you still need such coverage.

In such a situation, consider an individual term policy, which you get underwritten for any term length – 10, 20, or 30 years – with your premiums depending on underwriting and term length.

Another idea: Buy a large term policy individually and then supplement the maximum you can get through your employer.

That way, you always have you own policy regardless of what happens to your employment.

Income Replacement with Disability Insurance

Most individuals understand the need for life insurance. It pays a death benefit in the event a loved one, such as a spouse, dies prematurely. The death benefit is there to provide income for expenses, and to fund future expenses such as college or the surviving spouse's retirement.

However, a seldom though about income replacement tool is disability. Disability insurance should not be ignored, and arguably should be considered as a higher priority than life insurance. This is because statistically, an individual has a higher chance of becoming disabled, than dying prematurely. Especially if they're young.

Most disability policies are offered through an employer as benefit for employees. Typical policies provide 60-70% of income replacement in the event the covered employee becomes disabled. If you're self-employed, disability insurance is still recommended, and you may be able to deduct the premiums as a business expense.

When initially getting disability insurance, it's important to pay close attention to the definition of disability in the policy. This definition will determine whether the policy will pay or not, in the event of disability.

For example, a policy with a definition of "own occupation" will provide disability benefits in the event the insured becomes disabled and cannot perform the duties of their own occupation. This definition is critical for occupations such as surgeons, doctors, attorneys, and other professions that are highly specialized.

Another definition is "any occupation". A policy with this definition will only pay when it's deemed the insured cannot perform the duties of any occupation. This is a very strict definition and it's much more difficult for the insured to have the policy pay. Social Security's definition of disability is any occupation.

The premiums between the two definitions are different as well. With own occupation, the premium will be more expensive than any occupation. This is because the own occupation policy is more likely to pay in the event of a disability. But again, the extra premium is worth it for specialized occupations with high incomes to protect.

When deciding on a policy, be sure to check the elimination period. The elimination period is analogous to a "time deductible". In other words, how long the insured must wait after becoming disabled to receive benefits. Elimination periods range from 30 to 180 days. The longer the elimination period, the cheaper the premium and vice versa.

Choice of elimination period may coincide with how much is in the emergency fund (generally 3 to 6 months of expenses).

Finally, taxation of benefits will depend on how premiums are paid. If individuals pay premiums with after-tax dollars, then any benefits received are tax-free. If an employer pays the premiums, the employer can take a tax deduction and any benefits received are taxable to the employee. If benefits are paid by the employee on a pre-tax basis (as part of a benefit plan), then any benefits received are taxable.

Why You Should Consider Long Term Care Insurance

Long term care insurance is insurance that will pay if an individual needs caregiving due to several afflictions or diseases. For example, if an individual is suffering from Alzheimer's disease or dementia they made need round the clock care. Generally, that care is provided by family members, with many caregivers being daughters and spouses. Long term care insurance can help alleviate the caregiving burden on family members.

The costs for needing long term care can be expensive. Depending on the area of the country, care can range from $50,000 to $80,000 per year to stay in a nursing home and may run in the range of $20 to $30 per hour for care outside of the home. Based on the numbers above, long term care expenses can quickly drain an individual's retirement savings, or other assets that were planned for other uses.

Long term care insurance will help cover the costs of long-term care and may provide coverage for those costs in several settings. For example, Medicare specifically excludes coverage for custodial care (nursing home care). Long term care insurance will pay for these costs. Many individuals prefer not to go to a nursing home for care, some long-term care polices (called comprehensive) will pay for coverage needed in a facility or at home.

To qualify for long term care insurance an individual applying generally needs to be in good health and not showing any signs of chronic illness or mental incapacity. Once coverage is in place, most tax-qualified long-term care policies will start to pay benefits when the individual suffers from either substantial cognitive impairment (Alzheimer's or dementia) or is unable to perform 2 of 6 activities of daily living (ADLs).

The activities of daily living are eating, bathing, dressing, toileting, transferring from bed to chair, and continence. If a licensed health care professional deems an individual is unable to do 2 of the 6 ADLs for a period of 90 days, long term care insurance will "trigger" and start to pay benefits, subject to an elimination period.

When looking at the affordability of long-term care insurance premium a person or family needs to decide what the impact of not having care would be. Will an inheritance be lost or greatly diminished? Although not cheap, long term care insurance premiums are partially deductible (see IRS publication 502).

Siblings may even decide to purchase insurance on their parents in the event they live far away from their parents or to alleviate the caregiving burden on a sibling that may live nearby.

If you're age 50 or older, consider long term care insurance as part of your overall financial plan. While many people will choose to "self-fund" (pay for care out of other resources) others may choose to leverage the costs and transfer the risk of depleting assets to long term care insurance.

Chapter 2 – Debt

How to Tackle Debt

It can easily happen. Whether we're trying to keep up with the Joneses or investing in our education, sometimes debt can add up quickly. The good news is that debt can be erased. However, sometimes what we know we need to do is different from doing it.

Here's a game plan to start chipping away at your outstanding debt. With time and persistence, we can eliminate debt and increase our net worth.

Let's start with some definitions of debt. Debt is debt, but there is some debt that is better than others – call it good debt and bad debt. Mortgage debt is considered good debt (unless you bought more house than you can afford). Additionally, student loan debt is good debt (as you're investing in human capital), but interest rates can be higher than home debt.

Vehicle debt is generally bad, as you're borrowing money for a depreciating asset. Pay cash for your vehicles. Credit card debt is bad. It's debt that has no backing, no asset backing it. Credit card debt is deplorable as well. It's wise to reduce your credit card debt first (as it's usually the highest interest) followed by student debt, vehicle debt, then mortgage debt.

Start first on where you're spending your money. With a sheet of paper, make two lists. On the left-hand side, title this list "Needs". On the right-hand side, title this list "Wants". Usually, your wants will dwarf your needs. In this step, be honest with what your needs really are. For most people the basics are going to be shelter, food (groceries, not dining out), clothing, water, and utilities.

Grab last year's bank statement and circle or highlight all the needs. This will be mortgage/rent, groceries, utilities such as water and electricity, insurance and needed (not excess) clothing.

Now, start on the lists of wants. But instead of making a list from the top of your head, start going through your statements and listing the "wants" as they appear from what you've spent. Items such as a car payment, dining out, smartphone, coffee, TV/cable, etc., should be put down on the list of wants.

From there, determine what wants you're spending money on that can be given up to reduce your debt. If you find you're spending quite a bit dining out, consider taking that money and putting it toward your debt. The key becomes prioritizing. It's not uncommon (and in fact, it's quite easy) to find a few hundred dollars extra every month to plow into your debt.

Doing this exercise accomplishes a few things. First, it reduces your debt and builds your net worth. It also changes your habits and priorities. It forces you to think about your spending and whether a contemplated purchase will add any value to your life. It also provides guaranteed, risk-free returns. By eliminating debt, you are saving a ton of money in interest payments, effectively giving that return to yourself instead of a creditor.

Finally, it changes your habits. The good news is that once the debt is paid off, you can still treat the payments you were making as a bill. Only now, you're going to pay yourself first. For example, let's say you've been making an extra $400 payment to pay off your vehicle or credit cards. Once they're paid off, take that $400 and put it in your emergency fund, IRA or 401k. And keep making the payments. The good news is that you've already budgeted for it, only now the money goes in your pocket.

Paying Off Debt: A Guaranteed Rate of Return

Do you want a surefire return? Then whittle down what you owe, whether it's mortgage, automobile, boat, credit cards or college debt.

By paying down your debt, you guarantee a rate of return equal to the interest rate you pay on the debt. For some debt, it's a better return than the stock market might bring. Even if you have good credit, it's hard to come by an annual percentage rate of less than 15%, but a 15% annual gain in almost any investment is exceptionally good.

Bankrate has a handy a minimum payment calculator that shows just how pernicious credit card debt is. Many cards are now showing this in the fine print on their statements. For example, I put into the calculator a $10,000 balance at 15% interest and a minimum payment of $225. After just under 28 years of paying the minimum, I paid a total of $21,980. Pay off the card right away with $10,000, and right off the bat, you save nearly $12,000. If only it was so easy to find such a great rate of return on any other investment. Before you start sinking money into retirement accounts, a good idea is to get out of debt first.

Start on the debt with the highest interest rate. Typically, credit cards have the highest rates. Once you pay down that debt, move on to the next highest interest rate and so on.

Some people prefer to start on the smallest amount of debt first and go on from there. This strategy lets you build momentum by getting at least something paid off quickly. Then, you have one fewer account to pay the minimum on, and more money each month to pay off the costliest debt. You save more money paying down higher debt first, but if knocking down your smaller balances first gives you a feeling of accomplishment, that works just fine.

If you are struggling to find the money to get out of debt, you can get rid of luxury items you don't need, like cable TV or dining out, until your debt is gone. Try upping your payments in baby steps until you reach zero. You can tack on an additional 10% or more on what you currently pay and increase that percentage periodically until you can pay it off in full.

Should You Pay Off Your Mortgage Early?

As you pursue the American Dream of buying your first or next home, is it a good idea to pay down your mortgage – depleting part of your investment portfolio to eliminate the debt – or keep making the normal monthly loan payment and have more money in a stock market that offers potentially higher long-term returns? Both moves offer advantages depending on your unique situation.

Debt comes in different grades. Bad debt often includes credit-card balances and borrowing to pay for such purchases as gas, groceries, clothes or vacations. Necessary debt comprises costs of education or buying a house.

Many consider a mortgage about the only kind of a good debt. Many also fiercely advocate paying off debt, *any* debt, early. This is a wise choice when it comes to high-interest debts such as credit cards, student loans and other such loans.

The strategy may not always work for home-mortgage debt.

Generally, the younger you are when owning the home and the lower the interest rate on the mortgage, the more sense it makes to forgo extra mortgage payments and instead invest for potentially greater returns on the market.

Historically low interest rates and the potential tax deductibility of your mortgage interest may mean the return on paying down the mortgage early brings you up short compared to long-term gains in the market.

If older, you may want to pay down your mortgage early and own your home free and clear when you retire. The emotional satisfaction of dispensing with the mortgage expense in retirement and putting your former house payment to use elsewhere can feel sweet. Also, since you have less time to accumulate wealth via the market, paying off your home possibly gives you a greater return.

Another consideration: Do you need or want a safe, *guaranteed* return? Paying off debt early offers an excellent way to achieve such returns. And paying off mortgage debt can be considered part of your savings.

For example, if you and your spouse pay a 3.5% interest rate on your home and have 15 years left on your mortgage, paying off the mortgage early guarantees you at least 3.5% returns because you eliminate the debt's interest. You risk, on the other hand, missing out on potential market gains that may supersede the 3.5%.

Much debate over this question also hinges on whether the markets will – or can – continue delivering the high single-digit returns that investing gurus like Warren Buffett tout. No one can say for sure (and beware of any financial advisor who claims to have the skill) but the market's overall returns spanning the past half century speak for themselves – *and* beat 3.5%.

On the other hand, life's emergencies – loss of a job, an illness – spur many investors like you to tap their portfolios, often when markets and stock prices are lowest.

Again, this judgment call depends on your desire to get a guaranteed return or eliminate a debt. Reasonable home debt isn't bad. Your best move depends on your goals, situation and appetite for debt and risk.

Emergency Fund vs. Credit Card

In life we are faced with bad luck or simply things that go awry and inevitably cost us money. From a car needing repairs to the water heater going out, or an unexpected doctor bill; we don't plan for these to happen, but we can have a plan in place in case they do.

I recommend you have emergency funds because such events are going to happen. Sometimes I get the argument that an emergency fund isn't necessary if one has a credit card to simply pay for the unplanned expenses when they happen.

In an emergency, a credit card can come in handy as one may not have quick access to their cash. However, the flaw with thinking that a credit card can be used in place of an emergency fund lies here: How do you pay off the credit card?

The emergency may go away, but the credit card debt remains and the interest compounds not only on the debt but also the headache of the emergency the card was used to fund. Several emergencies in a small period of time can lead to high credit card debt – which is an emergency itself; only this emergency is preventable.

One thing to consider is to utilize both if necessary. In a pinch a credit card can come in handy if an emergency happens out of town, or as mentioned previously you don't have immediate access to your emergency fund.

The solution is once you have access to your emergency fund use that money to pay off the credit card that you just used for the emergency, and work on replenishing your fund.

Home Equity is Not a License to Spend

Many homeowners find themselves in a beneficial position a few or many years into their mortgage. As their payments continue, their mortgage balance gradually lessens and generally their home equity increases.

It may be tempting to view this increase in equity as a license to spend. In other words, individuals may be tempted to start spending on wants and no longer delay gratification.

A few arguments can be made in favor of using your home equity to make purchases. Such arguments include home remodels, purchasing vehicles, taking vacations, and paying for college. Additionally, some may argue that if interest rates are low, one could use home equity and invest in the stock market – profiting from the spread of market gains and the loan interest.

Let me give a few arguments against using your home's equity to make purchases. Regarding home improvements – why not save the money needed to make the improvements without a loan? These improvements can be done over time and do not diminish your net worth.

The same argument is true with vehicles and vacations. Save money to purchase vehicles (preferably used) and take vacations. And if you can't afford the vehicle or vacation – don't purchase it. Or better yet, think of a way to find cheaper transportation (bike, carpool, public) or take a cheaper vacation.

To combat the argument of using home equity to invest in the stock market, let me make one thing clear – market returns are not guaranteed. While there is the possibility to earn more than the interest rate on the equity loan, there is also the risk of losing money, yet still owing on the loan.

It makes very little sense to acquire debt, just to acquire more stuff. Additionally, real estate valuations are no guarantee. A home owner could take out a home equity loan and see the market value of the home drop (just like the stock market). Now the home owner is upside down – owing more money than the home is worth. This can create dire circumstances should the home need to be sold.

One argument I do favor regarding home equity is when considering a reverse mortgage. Reverse mortgages allow homeowners to tap the equity in their home to supplement their retirement income.

While reverse mortgages may be ideal for some, it's important to do your due diligence.

Reverse mortgages are covered later in this book.

The point is to delay gratification and keep working diligently to keep increasing net worth. Use home equity to build and increase wealth, not diminish it.

Avoiding Debt in College (For Students and Parents)

Junk food, credit cards and no parents watching – debt goes with weight gain in college like letterman jackets and dry leaves across the quad. Students must learn the dangers of over-spending with plastic, and here's how to keep down debt *and* your waistline.

This time of year, millions of students either embark from high school to college or return to campus from their summer. It's also when bad habits often result in freshman 15. This collegiate legend means that in the first few months of the new school year a student gains weight – maybe as much as 15 pounds – due to poor eating habits, stress and perhaps drinking.

I expand freshman 15 to also mean 15% of credit card debt. Like over-consuming food, over-consuming money on credit leads to bad habits and bad consequences.

When I was a college freshman the credit card offers poured in. What amazing copywriting, as if credit card companies wrote these offers just for me. The companies seemed to understand my situation; their words made perfect sense. Credit card companies pay copywriters thousands of dollars because that writing sells. Sell me it did. Had I not caught myself, I'd still have card debt at a rate of 15%.

Some campus traditions never change: Almost three quarters of undergrads and more than nine out of 10 graduate students use credit cards. Fewer than 10% of collegiate cardholders pay their full balance each month, only 15% have a clue about their interest rate and fewer than one in 10 know their rates, late fees and over-limit fees.

When college ends, most students and parents face heavy student loan debt. Compound that with debt from credit cards and many students get a first hard financial lesson after graduation.

To avoid the 15:

Pay yourself first. If you get student loans, scholarships, work study or grants, put a little aside. You'll be surprised. As the money grows you want to save more and spend less.

Carefully **consider applying for a credit card.** College students used to apply for retailers' charge cards to slowly build a credit rating. Credit runs freer now and a bank card might quickly ensnare you in debt. *Why* do you need the credit card? If you don't, don't apply. Chances are if you have to buy something on credit, you can't afford it. Consider cards specifically for students.

Talk to your parents about credit. They know more than you think. Parents – talk to your kids about credit. They'll listen more than you think.

Consider a card with no annual fees and a low credit limit. Use it just for emergencies, pay off your balance monthly and never spend more than you can pay off in one month.

Have an accountability partner. This could be parents with access to your account who can help monitor and ask questions. In many cases, parents also cosign for kids' first cards.

Establish an eating budget. Avoid dining out. Plan meals around your class schedule at the school's cafeteria. Pack a lunch and snacks if on campus and away from your dorm or apartment most of the day; this curbs binge eating and spending when you're hungry. Grocery shop when you're full, not hungry. Go home for holidays and breaks – you'll appreciate the food you once got for free.

Some financial moves dovetail with losing weight. Most colleges have free gyms and workout rooms for students, for example. Walk or bike to class to save on gas. If you must drive, park as far away as possible and walk – more exercise and fewer meters to feed. Take an exercise or nutrition class; you need these credits anyway and you might as well use the classes to your advantage.

Use your college years to establish good spending and eating habits. You'll graduate more prepared for success.

Student Loans Are Not Carte Blanche

For many college-bound and current college students, the arrival of the financial aid award can seem like winning the lottery. This sum of money is more than they've seen (in one sitting) in their entire lifetime.

The temptation to think of it as a "paycheck" rather than what it is – a liability – can often lead students to make less-than-optimal decisions when it comes to allocating those borrowed dollars.

When it comes to student debt it's helpful to think of it as just that – debt. This is money that is supposed to go towards the costs of higher education. When you are in the position of getting your award money, consider the consequences of using the money to finance unnecessary purchases. Remember, this is debt. It will have to be paid back someday; and with interest.

When you get your financial aid award check do a careful assessment of what your actual expenses for college are. These would be tuition, room and board and necessary food (meal plan), and expenses (books, lab fees). Your financial aid award should not finance a car, dining out with friends, the bar, or your spring break trips. It should only be used to fund the necessary expenses you must pay to attend college.

If there's a surplus of money left over, avoid the temptation to spend this money on unnecessary items. In fact, a very wise move would be to take any extra money and use it to pay off some of the student loan debt you've already incurred.

This will accomplish quite a few things. It will help boost your credit, it will reduce the total amount you owe when you graduate, and it will reduce the interest expense on the loans since the interest will be applied to a smaller principal balance.

Should you want extra income for the extras like dining out or spring break, consider getting a part-time job and use the money earned from the job to pay for those expenses. Or better yet, use that extra money to pay down your student loans.

College isn't cheap, but it doesn't have to leave you in enormous debt. Be smart with your financial aid award and only use what is necessary to stay in school. Use the extra to reduce the amount you've borrowed.

Should I Pay Off Debt or Save?

I often get quite a few debt questions from individuals ready to graduate college and start embarking on their first job. As is often the case, many of these individuals have varying amounts of student debt but also understand the importance of saving for retirement. Naturally, a common question is should they pay off student loans or save for retirement. Here's my take.

As I've mentioned previously, there are few ways to receive guaranteed returns. One of those ways is by paying down debt. This is an example of a guaranteed rate of return that is also risk free. By paying off a loan early, the interest that would have normally gone to the lender ends up in your own pocket. The good news is that the debt is retired faster, and you experienced zero volatility exposure compared to investing in the market.

On the other hand, what opportunity cost are you giving up by not investing in the market and allowing gains, dividends and interest a chance to compound over time? It's true that the earlier you start to save the more you can take advantage of time in the market and the miracle of compound interest.

We've all seen the examples of the difference between an individual that started investing early versus an individual getting a late start. In most cases the early investor comes out ahead.

Here are some things to consider if you find yourself in a similar situation. The first thing to do is assess your risk tolerance. In other words, are you capable of tolerating the market volatility (risk) that comes with investing outside of a risk-free return? If so, investing in the market may be something to consider.

Are you certain you can get a higher rate of return than the interest rate on your student loan? For example, if you have a student loan interest rate of 6.8% what are your chances of getting a return higher than 6.8% in the market? The odds may be in your favor in any given year and over longer time periods, but the odds of losing money also need to be considered (and you will lose money). Paying down this debt early guarantees you 6.8% return without risk. That's hard to beat.

Additionally, where do you plan on investing? For example, will you be investing in your employer's 401(k)? Does the 401(k) have a match? If you have access to a 401(k) and your employer provides matching contributions, I would recommend saving to your 401(k) to the point where you receive the full matching contribution. Consider the match free money - risk free money; another rarity when investing. Once you've committed to saving enough to take advantage of the full employer match, consider paying extra to your student loans or other debt.

After a while, your student loans will be paid off. Good for you! However, you will have a monthly loan payment that you've been budgeting for quite some time. Keep this monthly amount as part of your budget, and still treat it like a bill that's due every month. Only now, you're going to pay yourself. The good news is that you've already budgeted for it, but now you're simply allocating that money to your 401(k) or IRA. This is repetitive, but so important.

If you don't have an employer match, consider saving in your 401(k) anyway. Aim for 15-25% of your gross income and focus on putting any extra money to your student loans. In just a short period of time, you'll find that you're way ahead of the game when it comes to having little to no debt and quite a bit saved for retirement. It's simply a matter of prioritizing your money. Pay yourself first and live off the rest.

Chapter 3 – Saving

How to Save Money

You've heard the mantra to start saving money early, put something aside for retirement, or start accumulating a nest egg. As much as those mantras are good advice, sometimes an individual needs a specific direction on how to get started. Hopefully, this can provide some of that direction.

Whether you've just graduated high school, college, or have been working for several years, if you haven't started saving, there's still time to do so. It's never too late.

One of the first things an individual can do is simply look at what is coming in and what is coming out of their income. An easy way to do this is by looking at the last three month's bank statements. This will give an excellent representation of what income was coming in and what was being spent. From there, start separating needs from wants for your expenses. Be honest with yourself. Are you seeing expenses that are absolutely necessary?

Once you've identified expenses that aren't needs, tally them up for your monthly total. Here's the fun part. Since you've already budgeted for these items and you're already used to these being expenses, simply take that sum and have it put into a savings account (for an emergency fund) or open an IRA (for retirement). The nice thing about this step is it can be done automatically. At the beginning of each month you can have the sum automatically transferred to the savings or IRA and this reduces the "pain" of writing a check or the effort if physically transferring the money yourself.

Additionally, if you have access to a retirement plan at work, such as a 401(k), you can apply the same principles. Choose a percentage of your gross income that you'd like to save (15% is an excellent start) and have it taken out of your check before you're paid. This accomplishes two things: it takes care of the need to save and forces you to live off the rest. Furthermore, by saving a percentage of your income you automatically give yourself a raise to your retirement contributions any time you get a pay raise.

Saving doesn't have to be daunting. It can be hard to start and confusing on what approach to take. If you're willing to be honest with expenses (needs versus wants) and make your savings automatic, you may find it easier to save than you thought. And in just a few years' time, you'll have quite a bit of savings to show for it.

Pay Yourself First to Save

It's easy to save for retirement if you make it the first bill you pay. You can do this through fixed direct deposit, an employer retirement program or by getting on an automatic pay plan. It doesn't matter if it's only a small amount. What does matter is that you pay yourself first.

First, one of the easiest things you can do is take a portion of your paycheck and stick it right in the bank the day you get paid. If your employer allows direct deposit, take advantage of it.

Some employers even allow net and fixed direct deposit. Net direct deposit involves most of your paycheck going into your checking or savings account. Fixed direct deposit entails a small portion of the same paycheck going into a different account.

The beauty of this system is that you automatically put money into a separate savings account, and you never have to worry about remembering to save the money in the first place. After a few months, you may even forget about it until you receive your bank statement and see a nice sum already growing while you live comfortably on what's left.

If you get paid by paper check, you can set up a savings account with an automatic bill payment service. That way, when you cash your check and deposit it into your account, a certain sum is withdrawn from your checking account, into your savings account. This is the same as paying your bills automatically.

This way, you don't have to remember to consciously pay yourself. Treat your new savings account like a bill. Never miss a payment. Another method: Have your bank automatically wire the money to your individual retirement account or participate in your employer's 401(k), 403(b), 457, SEP, SIMPLE or profit-sharing plan.

The same concept applies where you dedicate a percentage or fixed amount from your paycheck every pay period. This saves money and lowers your taxes since these plans take money out on a pre-tax basis, meaning you're taxed on the sum left over after you've already saved.

I recommend starting out by saving 15% of your income. If that's a stretch for you, save 10% or even 5%. It's amazing how quickly it grows, and how easy it is to save even more.

Of course, money doesn't buy happiness, but can you remember how you felt the last time you found some stray cash on the street? Felt pretty good, didn't it? The same happens when you forget about what you're saving and find a tidy sum next time you open your statement.

Save by Dollar or Percentage?

When contributing to your employer-sponsored plan, you can choose to defer your income by a dollar or a percentage amount. The smart thing to do is to opt for whichever makes you save more.

An automatic deduction from your paycheck is an effective way to save for retirement regularly. When initially enrolling in a 401(k), 403(b), 457 or a savings incentive match plan for employees (SIMPLE), you elect how much, in dollar or percentage terms, you want to contribute each pay period.

Generally, the wiser decision is to choose the fixed percentage, because if you get a raise, your contribution automatically increases. You never have to worry about changing it during your time at this company.

For example, John starts a job earning $50,000 annually and decides to contribute 10% to his retirement plan, which is $5,000 per year. After a year, he gets a raise. Now he earns $55,000. The amount that goes into his retirement plan automatically increases to $5,500 annually.

If John selects the fixed amount, the good news is that he's at least saving. However, he saves $500 less per year. The gap widens if his income increases substantially over time unless he is diligent enough to change his contribution every time he gets a raise.

There's no universal rule for what percentage you should save, but you should at least contribute up to the percentage of your employer's match. And according to some studies those who saved more than $1 million in their 401(k)s on average deferred about 14% of their pay.

Choosing the fixed dollar amount has its benefit. You can spare yourself some math if you want to contribute the maximum to your 401(k). Simply divide the limit by the number of total yearly paychecks.

Let's assume Susan, 45, wants to give her retirement savings a boost by contributing the limit, which is $22,500 in 2023 and $25,500 for those over 50. She is paid 24 times per year. This equals a fixed dollar amount of $791 per paycheck. She can easily adjust the amount whenever contribution limits increase.

Another example of where a fixed dollar amount works is when a person contributes monthly to his or her individual retirement account. Most IRA custodians allow you to transfer a certain amount from a bank account into the IRA every month.

The traditional and Roth IRA contribution limits are $6,500. If you are over 50, you can make additional catch-up contributions of $1,000. Therefore, you can save up to $541.67 a month or $625 if you qualify for the catch-up.

How Much Do I Need to Save?

Frequently I'm asked how much should be socked away for retirement. Many people I talk to are concerned about having enough (a very common concern) for retirement and fear running out of money.

As much as I would love to give them a rock-solid answer and as much as they want a definitive answer, the true answer is that it depends – on several factors.

- How much do you plan to spend in retirement?

This question can be difficult to answer especially if you're young and can't contemplate an estimate of what expenses will be in retirement. For others, this may be more readily a number to come up with especially if they're close to retirement or in the peak accumulation years of their careers which is usually later in life.

- How much do you plan to give in retirement?

There may be a desire to give away some or all your wealth at retirement. This could range from a few thousand to several billion dollars (we're talking

Warren Buffett and Bill Gates wealth here). Naturally, the amount saved and accumulated over the working years needs to be greater than simply an amount needed to survive or enjoy retirement.

- What assets have you currently saved and accumulated?

If you're younger you're not looking at much, but here's the good news: time is on your side. You have much longer until retirement, but you also have the advantage of compounding returns as well as the potential of your human capital (your earnings over your lifetime) compounding as you advance in your career. If you're middle aged or older aged, there's a chance you have a home you may potentially downsize from or perhaps you'd consider a reverse mortgage. As you age, you have less human capital the closer you get to retirement, but hopefully that's been replaced with financial capital (what you've saved while working).

- How much do you plan on earning over your lifetime?

This is the $64,000 question – although I will say be careful with thinking that more money means more savings. Just by the numbers if a person makes more they can save more. But, it's true that the more someone makes the more they spend. I have seen very simple, frugal folks that turn out to be the millionaires next door and I have seen dual six-figure spouses live paycheck to paycheck and worry. A key point is this – when you start saving – and as you get raises, save more and continue to live frugally. It's amazing how fast your wealth will build.

Finding Extra Money to Save

Who can save for retirement these days? You can, if you know where to look and honestly assess what you can live without.

Here's a fun exercise I do with my undergraduate students. I ask my entire class to make a list of the wants (not needs) on which they frequently spend money. Answers vary from smartphones, cable and satellite TV, coffee shops and beverages (I don't press them on specifics on that one) to such grooming costs as hair coloring, pedicures, and the like.

Here are my students' monthly expenses, on average:

- Smartphone service: $150
- TV: $100
- Eating out: $150
- Coffee: $75
- Other beverages: $200
- Appearance: $100

The above amounts total $775 monthly, $9,300 annually.

These are college students; not one holds a full-time job, though many do work part time. They are arguably on the low end of the spectrum of annual income. I mention this only to clarify that, if they can sock away money, so can almost everyone else.

Now, the maximum yearly contribution to an individual retirement account for 2023 is $6,500 ($7,000 for those 50 and older). In other words, the young adults in my class can max out an annual IRA contribution and still enjoy $2,800 left over to invest elsewhere.

Let's say one of my students can only spare half that extra cash to invest but does have 40 years to invest before retiring. Assuming that amount stays constant – if anything it's likely to grow as the student's career progresses – four decades of investing $1,650 per year with a conservative annual return of 4% results in over $150,000 saved for the golden years.

If college students can find the money, anyone can. So how do you get started?

First, look at your last three months' bank statements for a representative sample of where you spend money. I recommend using past statements; keeping track of upcoming expenditures will likely skew the data, since you'll likely control spending once you start tracking it.

On your statements, separate the wants from the needs. Be honest with yourself. Do you need or want an expensive smartphone? What about the top tier of cable TV?

Sometimes separating needs from wants comes hard. My students find smartphones a big point of contention: Many students, initially claiming to need the devices, eventually admit that smartphones aren't necessities.

Other examples: Car maintenance might be a need because you drive to get to work; your new car sound system is a want. You need a new stove because your old one quit and you cook at home (saving money on eating out, incidentally); a complete new set of bakeware is a want.

Force yourself to distinguish the needs you require to live and survive from the expenditures on what you merely want. Total your wants expenditures from the last three months and divide by three to get your average monthly spending on wants.

Now, transfer that spending to your IRA. In fact, have your monthly IRA contribution automatically deducted from your bank account. That way you never see the money until retirement – when you'll need it.

How Much is 1%?

A penny saved is a penny earned and penny-pincher are two common terms that are used to describe someone that is most likely frugal. I would admit I am one of those individuals that aspire to both phrases – and it's not out of accident.

I am one of those folks who will pick up a penny (heads or tails showing – no superstitions here) when walking down the street and put it in my pocket. That penny, nickel, or quarter (in rare cases a one-dollar bill or even higher) will usually make its way into my piggy bank or more likely one of my daughters' porcelain pigs.

I pick up the loose change for one of two reasons:

- It's literally *free* money. To not pick it up is asinine.
- Little amounts add up.

Think of it this way – a penny is 1% of a dollar. A dollar is 1% of a hundred dollars, and a hundred dollars is 1% of ten-thousand dollars. 1% seems small, but 1% added and then compounded grows exponentially.

When it comes to saving an extra 1% - it's easy. If you make $50,000 a year, 1% of that is $500. Next year, save another 1% (for a total of 2%) and now you're saving $1,000. And that's annually. Broken down into monthly, that's about $42 per month – or $10.50 a week – or $1.50 a day – or 6 pennies an hour.

If we look at the bigger chunks when it comes to savings – the amount can seem daunting, but when we break it down – in this case literally 1%, it becomes much more doable.

If you're not saving now, commit to saving 1%. If you're currently saving, save 1% more. It might not seem like much, but remember that avalanches are caused by many, many little snowflakes.

How to Save On Holiday Spending

When Thanksgiving comes and goes and before we know it the Holidays upon us. For many people, this time of year means the giving and exchanging of gifts to family, friends, and loved ones. It also means people may worry about their spending over the Holiday season; with concerns of how to budget, going over budget, or amassing unwanted amounts of credit card debt.

Here are some ideas to help keep your Holiday spending in check to stick to your budget and avoid the trap of credit card debt – the gift that keeps on giving.

- Create a spending plan and stick to it. Have a budget when it comes to what you will spend on gifts for the Holidays. It may be tempting to spend more than this budget when we see additional gifts we'd like to give, or we feel guilty that what we've purchased isn't enough for the person the gift is intended for. Sticking to your budget reduces the temptation to spend money you don't have.

- Consider shopping earlier in the year. Rather than wait until the last minute, consider doing your shopping throughout the year. Items can be purchased throughout the year when they're on sale, and perhaps when emotions are less likely to influence last-minute spending.

- Save for your Holiday gifts throughout the year. Many banks and credit unions offer a Holiday account where you can save your money specifically for the Holidays. Then, when it's time to purchase gifts, the money is already there, budgeted for, and ready to be used for its intended purpose. Avoid department store credit card offers to finance your spending.

- Communicate expectations. If things are tight or your budget is small, consider explaining this to your family. In most cases, family and friends will be completely understanding of the situation and will often suggest not giving them anything at all. Conversely, they may feel

relieved when you tell them the same thing –
a gift isn't necessary.

- If a friend or family member mentions that
  they would rather not get a gift, consider
  taking that comment seriously. Granted, this
  is difficult to do as the act of giving gifts is an
  expression of love and appreciation. Respect
  their request. Perhaps in lieu of a gift, you
  write a nice card or note of appreciation to
  them. Another idea is to donate in their name
  to a charity or organization they're involved in
  or have interest.

- Combination gifting. Family members can
  pool their gift money to give a bigger gift to
  their loved ones. This allows family members
  to participate in giving, without feeling bad
  that they can't give as much. Additionally, the
  folks pooling their money should agree on the
  amount each person will contribute. Those
  with higher incomes or who've done better
  planning should not be expected to contribute
  the most. It should remain equal. It also
  means that those with more money to give
  should stick to the agreed upon amount to

avoid contention and ill-feelings from those who can't give more.

- Giving is not quid pro quo. If you receive a gift, be thankful. If you didn't plan on giving to the person who gave a gift, consider not doing so, but perhaps send a note of thanks. If you give, don't expect anything in return. Giving is self-less.

Am I Saving Too Much?

This is in response to a question an individual had for me when I was meeting with them some time ago. The question they had for me was if they were saving too much money.

The reason they asked is that after a conversation with friends of theirs, the friends had collectively said she was saving too much money for retirement. Currently, this 25-year-old was saving 26% of her income for retirement! My verbal response was a firm, "Well done!" My internal response was, *"Get some new friends."*

Her friends were trying to convince her that 10% was more than enough to save for retirement at such a young age. While 10% is a decent amount to put away, 26% is even better. In addition, this young lady was already *used* to saving 26% of her income. And it wasn't straining her financially.

This is what I told her. I recommended that she keep saving the same amount and gave her some reasons why. The first reason is that once she reduced the amount to say, 10% of her income, she would have an extremely difficult time increasing it in the future. Psychologically, she would be used to spending that money on something else and would see an increase as a "sacrifice" that would put strain on her income.

Second, we discussed the time value of money. Like any finance nerd I grabbed my financial calculator and went to work. Based on her income of $50,000 and current investment of $25,000 already in her plan, I took 26% of her income ($13,000) and invested that annual payment at 6% for 30 years. This turns out to be just over $1.17 *million* dollars (not accounting for any annual raises). Next, I reduced the annual contribution to just $5,000 (10%) of her income (again, not accounting for raises). In 30 years, her nest egg dropped to just under $539,000 – less than half of what she's currently on track to have.

Finally, and respectfully, I asked if her friends were willing to hand her a check at retirement for the difference. In other words, I asked if she was confident her friends would hand her a check in 30 years for $631,000 as congratulations for taking their advice.

She simply smiled and shook her head no.

You can never save too much.

Chapter 4 – Investing

How to Invest (In the Market)

Occasionally, I get asked: "Did you see what the market did today?" or "How did the market do today?" To be honest, I'd love to use the line from the movie *Gone with the Wind*; "Frankly my dear, I don't give a damn."

Professionally, my response is usually "I couldn't tell you" or "I don't follow the market."

The response is not meant to be rude or abrupt, but more to simply say that for most investors (myself included); they shouldn't be worried about what the market is doing on a day to day basis. This is especially true for the Dow Jones Industrial Average. A price weighted index of 30 stocks is hardly representative of the market, yet it's what most people think and refer to as "the market" when they ask the questions above or read the news.

The other reason is when you think of it, do we really have control over the market? In other words, what's the sense in worrying about something that's beyond our control? Instead, we can focus on what we can control. One of those is expenses. The other is diversification. The good news is that both are easy to control and easy to implement.

As the title says, this is how most individuals can and should invest. Leave worrying about market fluctuations to individuals who think they can beat the market, but very rarely do consistently.

How to Control Expenses

One of the best ways to control expenses is to find passively managed funds such as index funds. Index funds simply buy a market basket of securities. Since they represent a market index (such as the S&P 500, the bond market, real estate market, etc.) they generally don't have a manager actively buying and selling securities to beat the market. The more a manager actively trades, the more expenses increase – and lower investors' returns.

Not all index funds are created equal. This is something I wrote about in the past. Investors should look for index funds that are no-load (do not pay the broker an up-front commission) and with expense ratios of .5% (1/2 of 1%) or less. Two companies that offer very inexpensive index fund options are Vanguard and Fidelity. Once you've selected which company you're going to use it's now time for the next step.

How to Diversify

When it comes to diversification, investors should first consider which assets classes they will select to invest and diversify into. Asset allocation and diversification are different. Asset allocation means selection from asset classes such as stocks, bonds, REITs, commodities, etc. Diversification means spreading your investment selection among a particular asset class. Once an investor has picked their asset classes the choice of funds from the above two providers becomes easy.

An investor can have excellent asset allocation and diversification with only a few funds in their portfolio. For example, an investor could choose a total stock market index fund, total bond market index fund, an international index fund, and a REIT index fund and arguably never have to look at it again except to rebalance occasionally. The weights of the funds (percent of the portfolio dedicated to each fund) need to be determine by the investor and may solicit the help of a competent financial planner. Financial planning professionals can assist the client with understanding their appetite for risk, goals, time horizon, and tax implications of their investments.

It's been said that diversification is the only free lunch in investing. That is, according to Modern

Portfolio Theory investors can combine individually risky assets while lowering the overall risk in the portfolio.

I'd love to tell you that investing is rocket surgery, but it isn't. The industry can make it complicated and I would argue that the more complicated, the less benefit to investors. Investors should focus on what they can control; expenses and diversification; and get competent professional advice when necessary.

Can You Beat the Market?

The words "beat the market" appear from time to time either as part of an investment strategy, conversation, or a combination of both. Investors can be lured by the phrase in the hopes of achieving returns superior than the market or "above average".

When we refer to the market, we're generally referring to a benchmark such as the Dow Jones Industrial Average (The Dow) or the S&P 500. First off, I'd like to offer a bit of clarity before attempting to answer the titular question. If fact, I'd like to ask two questions and answer both – because they will have different answers, even though they look similar.

First, I think it's appropriate to ask this question:

Can the market be beaten?

To which I answer, yes. The market can be beat, and there are times where certain investments, funds, and managers have done better than the market.

The second question I'd like to ask is found in the title:

*Can **you** beat the market?*

To which I answer, likely no, and good luck if you try.

Do you see the similarities in the questions? Both have inferences of outperforming the market, but the second question asks the reader specifically. In other words, the market can be beat, and gets beaten every year. The odds are, *you* won't do it.

The reason it's hard to beat the market is information, or lack of it. Do you have access to the information that billion-dollar firms have access to – and the speed in which they can access it?

Do you have the money and time to invest in company analysis, research, and due diligence?

Finally (and maybe most important), do you have the temperament to try to beat the market? By temperament I mean the patience, tolerance, grit, and self-control. These are needed to stay in an investment when it's getting beat up as well as the wisdom to sell or buy when necessary.

And then there are the costs of trying to beat the market – fees, commissions, etc., all eat into returns. The market doesn't have to contend with them.

While not impossible, beating the market is a gargantuan battle. And to do so consistently is extremely difficult. Let me also leave you with some proof. Every year S&P releases information on how US equity funds did relative to their benchmark (the market). You can find the report by going to https://us.spindices.com/spiva/#/

If you can't beat the market, simply join it. This is done through index investing.

Asset Allocation Vs. Diversification

The question of how we array our investments is vital to our future financial well-being. The key to this is knowing the different between asset allocation and diversification

Some think that asset allocation and diversification are the same. They aren't. An investor may have excellent diversification but poor asset allocation and vice versa. To keep unnecessary risks to a minimum, we need both.

Let's start with asset allocation. This refers to the actual act of investing in different categories of investments, called asset classes. That is, we pick which assets we want to have in our portfolio. Generally, investors choose from stocks (equities), bonds (fixed income), cash, commodities and real estate.

Diversification, on the other hand, is the process of balancing these classes – and within these classes – so they offset one another amid ever-changing market conditions.

Suppose an investor buys one single stock, one bond, holds one dollar, one ounce of gold and owns a home, this is an example of excellent allocation across all the asset classes. However, the diversification is terrible.

Assume we have a total of $100 ($20 each) in the five asset classes. If the company issuing the stock goes bankrupt, we immediately lose 20% of the portfolio and now hold a total of $80. This, of course, assumes that the rest of the market does not change.

The following year, the company that issued the bond defaults on its debt and cannot repay the bondholders. Now, our portfolio is worth only $60, a 40% loss in two years. The next year gold doubles, as does real estate, which brings the portfolio back to a total of $100 ($40 in gold, $40 in real estate and $20 in cash). We are back where we started financially but with fewer asset class categories.

Then, stocks and bonds soar. Since we lost our stock and bond exposure when they tanked, we miss a huge opportunity. Not to mention that cash lost money (purchasing power) due to inflation.

As an alternative, if we still choose the same asset classes, but diversify within those asset classes, we have some protection against market volatility. For example, we don't choose just one stock, but several hundred or thousand stocks to hold – divided among small-capitalization, mid-cap, large-cap and international. Similarly, instead of one bond, we hold many short-term, intermediate and long-term corporate bonds, as well as Treasuries. The same is true for commodities (holding not only gold, but silver, etc.) and real estate.

How do we buy all this? Easy – mutual funds or exchange-traded funds. When we put money into a mutual fund or an ETF, we invest in hundreds of securities all at once.

To keep expenses low, choose index funds. They are a type of mutual fund that tracks the performance of an index. For the stock exposure, we can buy a total stock market index fund. There is also a total bond market index fund, a commodity index fund and a real estate investment trust (REIT) index fund. These funds not only accomplish broad asset allocation but provide excellent diversification within the asset's classes.

This way, even if a company declared bankruptcy, and its stock and bonds become worthless, it won't ruin our portfolio.

Diversify, Diversify, Diversify

Market predictions are just guessing. To prevent your entire portfolio from sinking in one market swoon, diversify.

For every person who says stocks will have a meteoric rise this year, there are just as many that say you should avoid them. You hear some saying that bonds are doomed, while others sing their praises. Buy gold, sell gold; buy real estate, sell real estate. The point is neither you nor I (or anyone else) can *accurately* predict which does well, which does horribly, or which does better than others.

Of course, from time to time, some people guess right. They interpret their luck as superior knowledge, as if they knew more than the market does. Hindsight is 20/20, but foresight is 20/200. Often, these folks make several *hundred* guesses and only brag about the one or two they get right, ignoring the many others they get wrong.

Forget about trying to predict which investment is the winner or the loser. You never know for sure. Here's one thing to keep in mind for today and beyond: diversification.

A diversified portfolio contains investments from different classes – stocks, bonds, real estate and commodities. The purpose of this strategy is reducing risk. If one asset class performs poorly, others may offset the loss. Diversification doesn't mean you don't lose money, but at least, it offers some downside protection.

With a diversified portfolio, you should expect gains and losses in every asset class you own. Rarely do all asset classes move in the same direction together. If *all* your investments go up at the same time and down at the same time, you're not properly diversified. If, in a bull market, all you see is spectacular gains and little losses – be very concerned.

It's not enough you are diversified across asset classes; you also must diversify within them. Don't buy one stock based on opinions that are essentially guesses. Buy broad-based index funds, which contain a lot of different types of stocks.

You may see articles that tell you to invest like Warren Buffett, the investing legend who is known to be a critic of diversification. Sorry to break it to you, but you are not the Oracle of Omaha, nor can you ever invest like he does. After all, unlike Buffett, you probably don't have a few extra billions of dollars to buy companies.

If you look at the holdings of his investment company, Berkshire Hathaway, there's actually plenty of diversification, from insurers to underwear companies. Berkshire Hathaway is like an index fund.

And that's what you should think like when you invest. Work with trusted advisors and invest wisely in different asset classes with excellent diversification among those asset classes.

Correlation, Risk, and Diversification (A Bit Technical)

By now you understand the importance of asset allocation and diversification. Without getting too technical, the reason why asset allocation is important is due to correlation (often signified by the Greek letter rho or ρ) to the overall stock market.

Assets with a correlation of +1 (perfect positive), move identically to each other. That is, when one asset moves in a direction, the other moves in the exact same fashion. Assets with a correlation of -1 (perfect negative), move exactly opposite of each other. That is, when one asset class zigs, the other asset class zags.

The benefits of diversification begin anytime correlation is less than +1. For example, a portfolio with two securities with a correlation of .89 will move similar to each other, but not exactly the same. Thus, there is a diversification benefit. In other words, both securities may fall in a market downturn, but one may fall further than the other. The other security dropped, but not as bad as its counterpart.

The reason correlation among asset classes is important is because it allows investors to create portfolios with different asset classes, while lowering risk. This is also why diversification works. One of the caveats of diversification is that the more diversified we are, we can eliminate certain risks. We can improve our risk-adjusted returns. This is one of the finer points discovered by Dr. Harry Markowitz in his work developing Modern Portfolio Theory.

Investors are subject to two broad categories of risk when investing; systematic risk and unsystematic risk. Systematic risk is undiversifiable. In other words, systematic risk cannot be eliminated no matter how much an investor diversifies. This risk is also called economy-based risk, market risk, reinvestment rate risk, exchange rate risk, and interest rate risk.

Unsystematic risk is risk that can be eliminated through proper diversification. Unsystematic risk includes accounting risk, business risk, country risk, default risk, financial risk and government risk. We don't have to invest in just one business, or one country.

The graph below illustrates the more securities we add to a portfolio the lower the risk becomes – up to a certain point. That point is when the curved line nearly touches, but never does, the market risk line. This asymptotic relationship means that we can get very close to the market risk line, but never eliminate market risk. Market risk is *always* present.

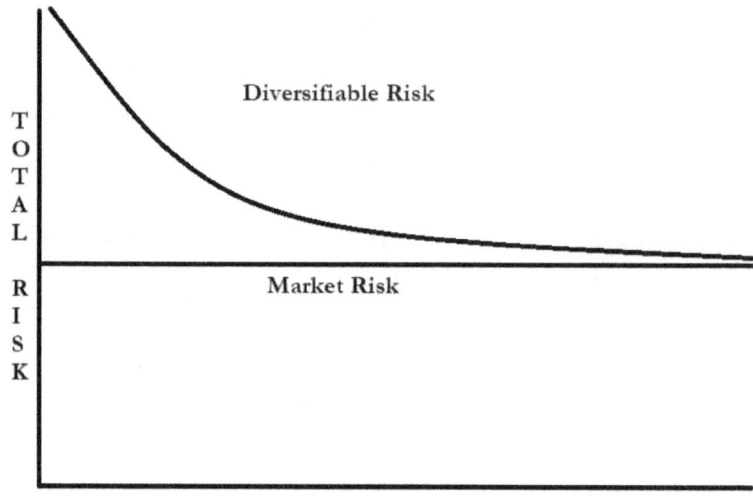

Number of Stocks (Bonds) In Portfolio

A key point for investors to understand is that diversification *reduces* but does not *eliminate* risk. Investors should understand that there will always be risk and that there's no such thing as a riskless asset.

Another consideration that investors must understand is that if they are properly diversified, they will not perform the same as the market in a bull market. In other words, if the S&P 500 increases 30% in any given year, the investor's portfolio should not do the same. The same is true in a bear market. A 30% decline in the S&P 500 should not mirror the investor's portfolio. If all an investor's investments go up together and down together, they're not properly diversified. A well-diversified portfolio will have some assets increase while others decrease.

This can be a tough pill to swallow when the market is seeing record gains and our portfolios seem to be struggling to keep up. Well-diversified investors are (somewhat) comforted when the market drops heavily and don't see their own portfolios suffer as greatly.

What is Risk Tolerance?

What is risk tolerance and why is it important to investors? As an investor you've probably been asked this question by yourself, or your financial advisor. It's not an easy question to answer and not a question that should be answered with one word or a quick sentence.

Risk tolerance is simply your appetite for risk. Some investors have little appetite for risk and their stomach churns when they think about losing money in the market. These investors are considered risk averse or risk *intolerant*.

Other investors aren't really concerned about the ups and downs of the market and are willing to accept these market gyrations to receive the benefit of potentially higher returns. For these investors to receive higher returns they must be willing to accept more risk for those returns. In other words, these investors are risk *tolerant*.

You can see the pattern. Risk averse investors sacrifice returns for lower risk. Risk tolerant investors take more risk in exchange for higher returns. This is called the risk-return trade-off.

This concept is important for several reasons. The first is that it helps you properly line up the correct investment portfolio for your objectives. A risk averse investor will be more at ease in a low-risk portfolio with fewer stocks, have more exposure to high-quality bonds and cash. A risk tolerant investor would be more tolerant of risk – such as more exposure to stocks, and other riskier assets.

Determining your appetite for risk isn't that easy. There are several risk tolerance questionnaires used by various companies and professionals to help you narrow down your risk tolerance. This is hard to do depending on the day – literally!

The reason why is because on any given day the market could be way up, way down, or flat. Someone who is really risk averse may *feel* risk tolerant in a bull (up) market (isn't everybody?), but that same person will run for the antacids the second the market drops; which leads to this point:

Investors' real appetite for risk appears in bear (down) markets.

What can you do? Find a professional that asks a lot of questions and takes the time to get to know you. Yes, a risk tolerance questionnaire can be used and is a good thing, but the questionnaire should be only a piece of the conversation. You can ask yourself questions too.

Imagine you have $100,000 invested and in two weeks it grows to $150,000. How do you feel? In another two weeks it plummets to $75,000. Now how do you feel?

You answer may offer insight as to how tolerant you are of risk.

Perception and Reality

Investors, like all humans, are biased toward making decisions based on the information at hand. But too often you get a distorted view of reality and that can lead to bad money behavior. Here's how to overcome this perceptual problem.

Psychologists Daniel Kahneman and Amos Tversky coined the term availability bias: our tendency to use the information available to us to make quick judgments.

For example, if all your friends and co-workers own a smartphone, you probably figure that most people have smartphones. In reality, not even half of Americans own one. That's a problem if you expect to deal with customers using an app on their mobile screens. Or you might have an irrational fear of flying thanks to news reports of a recent plane crash. Statistically, you are safer traveling in a plane than in a car. So you stick to time-consuming ground transportation.

When it comes to investing, availability bias can cause bad decisions. My grandmother, for instance, grew up during the Great Depression. She was an extremely frugal person. She saved everything. She even washed and reused zippered sandwich bags.

She also never invested or saved one cent in the market. As a child she saw what the market did to her friends and family – and she wanted no part of it. There were many other factors that led to the Depression, but according to the information she had readily available to her, it was the market's fault. That meant that she had very few assets to give her a comfortable living in her old age.

Fast forward roughly 90 years and people have very similar feelings in the aftermath of the Great Recession. People who lost half of their net worth in 2008 or sold their portfolio at the bottom in 2009 feel a lot like my grandmother, apprehensive about investing. A newly graduated college student who just landed a great job in a growing field and watched his wealth grow in the company 401(k) while the Dow Jones Industrial Average breached 25,000 points 10 years later probably doesn't feel the same way.

Much of our availability bias stems from what we read, what we hear and who we associate with. It's extremely difficult to go against the grain. This is why co-workers invest in the same funds in their company retirement plan yet have completely different ages and goals.

Another example where availability bias wreaks havoc on our portfolios is our tendency to chase returns. This is when an investor buys a stock or fund based on how well it performed in the past.

Looking at the information available, he or she reasons that it's a good bet. We are much less likely to buy a fund with negative returns in recent years.

But there is a reason brokers are careful to say that past performance doesn't equate to future growth. Today's winner might be tomorrow's loser. Chasing returns is a very efficient way to continually buy high and sell low.

Take Bank of America. In 2011, it was the worst performer in the Dow. In 2012, it gained 45%, making it the best performer in the index.

How can investors avoid falling into the availability bias trap?

Educate yourself. Do your due diligence and learn more about your investments, your proposed investments and why you're making the decision you're about to make.

Know your time horizon. A lot of your investment decisions come from what your time frame is for your investment. 30 years until retirement and 30 years into retirement are two very different points in people's lives.

Work with a professional advisor. Consulting with a professional can help you keep your emotions in check, ask questions and deliver insight you might not have thought of.

Relax. Rome wasn't built in a day and neither is your portfolio. Wealth is built over time, and markets wax and wane.

The Folly of Chasing Returns

The stock market can have a wonderful year and the next year end up going in the opposite direction. The reversal alone is a sobering warning about how chasing hot investments is a very bad idea. Peering inside the psychology of markets shows why.

In bullish market years, stories abound of smart gambles – er, investments – that pay off royally. One firm that bets heavily on Japanese stocks performs very well, another investor bets against gold and achieves glamorous returns and a hedge fund that bets on U.S. stocks looks like a god among mortals.

But that's the problem with these scenarios. We are mortal.

By picking up any financial magazine that reports on funds or stock returns, you see examples of mutual funds, stocks and bonds that either beat or trail their counterparts. For example, U.S. stocks do very well in a given year – so a domestic large capitalization fund looks amazing, based on what it did for that year.

Herein lies the problem; the publication is reporting what the fund *did*, not what it will *do*.

Investors who chase returns fall prey to the thinking that past returns are indicative of future results, when we know that that's not the case. There's no guarantee that the fund, stock or bond will increase in value, and there's no guarantee that it will decline. We just don't know.

There may be a good chance that a top-returning fund is going to go down, although it may not happen right away. The reason is that when the publications show the funds with amazing returns, there are some people who flock to them, chasing returns, and prices temporarily increase.

What happens next is that several long-term investors in the fortunate fund sell – and sell a lot. Naturally, when there's quite a bit of selling fund prices drop, and so do the returns of those who jumped into the hot fund, expecting more increases.

Another reason prices drop is mean reversion. Simply stated, this concept holds that a fund's prices will move toward their average over time. A simple, but exaggerated, example: Say a fund's average return is 10% over 20 years. In one year it returns 40%, which is very respectable. However, according to mean reversion, expect (although there's no guarantee as to when) that, at some point, the fund's return declines, either gradually or suddenly. It gets back to its average of 10%.

Another way to look at this concept is standard deviation, which measures how much something flip-flops around an average. To keep things easy, let's say this fund has a standard deviation of 10% also. With an average return of 10% and a high of 40%, it means that this fund went three standard deviations *above* its average. This means that it could also go three standard deviations *below* the average or deliver a negative 20% return.

Without getting too mathematical or statistical, the upshot is that this fund flip-flops a lot. If it logged a 40% return in the last year, there's a good chance it could flop going forward.

Rather than chasing returns a wise choice is to invest broadly among asset classes and diversify accordingly. An excellent way to do this is through indexing – buying index funds of different asset classes (such as stock, bonds real estate and international stocks and bonds). This helps you avoid chasing returns and helps you accept that certain asset classes will rise and others will fall.

But the combination of many securities in one portfolio not only lowers overall portfolio risk, but also prevents an investor from chasing the next big fund – whose lush returns *already happened.*

Be Careful of Average Returns

When saving and investing for retirement many individuals will consider how much they can save, how much they need at retirement, and how long they have to save until retirement.

Essentially, all the ingredients in the previous paragraph boil down to a phrase mentioned many times in in finance, investing, and business: the time value of money.

The time value of money helps individuals and businesses figure out how much they need to save, earn, and spend in order to achieve certain financial goals. What it boils down to is what is a dollar worth, if not spent today, and instead invested and allowed to grow for tomorrow (the future).

The essential components of a time value of money calculation are present value (PV), payments (PMT), future value (FV), interest rate (I) and number of periods (N).

Chances are throughout your lifetime you may have done this type of calculation yourself when calculating how much you need to save for retirement or how much you will have when you reach retirement.

For example, if you can save $500 per month (PMT) for 30 years (N) and if you can earn 8% (I) on your investment you'll have roughly $745,000 (FV).

Some of you already notice the flaw in this equation: we're assuming an average return of 8%. This means that we're assuming our investments earn 8% per year! Here's the problem with this assumption. Let's say that our goal is still $745,000 for retirement and the same number of years apply. Assume our average return is only 5%. What happens to how much we have to save monthly? We now have to save $895 instead of $500.

We see that as our rate of return drops, we must contribute *more*. And what happens when we assume too high a rate of return? Let's use 10% in our above example. We now only need to save about $330 per month to hit our goal. Perfect!

Wrong!
(tangelo)

This is a big problem with not only saving for retirement, but I would also argue (ahem) a big reason why some public pensions are in trouble. Pensions don't have to save as much for their future liabilities to pensioners (retired employees) when they have higher expected rates of return.

I won't bore you with why this strategy is futile; simply re-read the last couple of paragraphs to get the idea.

M. Barton Waring in his book *Pension Finance* as well as Jim Otar in his book *Unveiling the Retirement Myth* write extensively on this concept. Mr. Waring says that pensions assuming a higher expected return "because that's what they can expect in the long-term" is ludicrous. Mr. Otar mentions that "averages don't apply to individuals" – meaning what if we did get our 8% for 29 years, but lost 50% in year 30?

Both gentlemen are correct.

My advice: use a smaller rate of return. You'll have to save more, but it will cause you to rely less on "averages" and more on what you can control – your ability to save.

Mutual Funds and ETFs – A Great Choice for Your Portfolio

Investing in individual stocks* is an option for your portfolio. However, investing in stocks involves a lot of diligence, research, and discipline. Many of us don't have the time, money, or fortitude to carry through with an investment plan that includes individual stocks.

Additionally, stock picking can lead to additional stress if you find yourself constantly (daily) looking at your stocks and worrying if you should buy, sell, or hold. If you think you're the type of person who could unemotionally buy and sell stocks for your portfolio and remain consistent in doing so, then you may be the rare investor where this could be a viable option.

Building a portfolio of stocks also means you must purchase enough stocks – and enough different types of stocks – to have adequate diversification to reduce your risk compared to owning just one or a few companies. This can be difficult to do if your money is limited or the prices of the companies you've researched are out of your budget (e.g. as of this writing, Berkshire Hathaway A shares are trading at just over $300,000 *per share*).

*Or individual bonds

Here's where investing in mutual funds and ETFs (exchange traded funds) can be beneficial. Some of the advantages of investing in mutual funds or ETFs include instant diversification, economies of scale, professional management, and (generally) lower expenses.

Instant Diversification – Unlike investing in several single stocks to achieve diversification, purchasing just one share of a mutual fund or ETF gives you exposure to hundreds, if not thousands of different companies.

Depending on the goal of the fund (large, medium, or small company, US, international, bond, etc.) it will hold a sample of the companies that make up the investment allocation the fund is trying to achieve.

Let's say you want to invest in the S&P 500 – an index of roughly 500 larger US companies. Purchasing a fund replicating the S&P 500 would get you access to over 500 companies with only one share! The same would be true for a bond fund, international fund; you get the point.

Economies of Scale – This means that by using mutual funds or ETFs allows you to have access to many companies for less than the cost of purchasing them separately. Looking at our S&P 500 example, an investor purchasing individual stocks would have to buy over 500 different stocks to replicate this index. Very expensive to do.

By purchasing a mutual fund or ETF replicating the S&P 500, the investor gets exposure to over 500 companies, with only 1 share of the fund, for substantially less money.

Professional Management – Investing in mutual funds or ETFs gives you access to professional money managers whose job it is to monitor the portfolio of stocks so you don't have to. Often fund managers have extensive experience, education, and certifications that qualify them to manage the fund(s) they oversee. This alleviates you from the stress of constantly looking at your investments (which you shouldn't do anyway).

Depending on the type of fund (actively versus passively managed), the fund may have more than one manager and may have more expenses due to the goal of the fund (e.g. funds that try to beat the market typically charge more).

Lower Expenses – In many cases investing in mutual funds or ETFs carries lower expenses. In additional to requiring less money to invest in more companies, choosing lower expense funds means that more of your money is working for you. You should consider looking for funds that have expense ratios of .5% (one-half of 1 percent) or less. This should be easy to do by choosing index mutual funds or ETFs.

What An Active Fund Manager Won't Tell You

Many people reading this will have some experience with mutual funds. Whether part of your IRA, 401(k), or other savings vehicle mutual funds play a key role in helping people achieve their savings goals with access to a wide variety of companies and diversification along with professional management.

By professional management we mean an individual or team of managers that run the day to day activities of the fund such as buying and selling of stocks and bonds as well as running financial analyses of the different companies whose stock they are looking at adding to or selling from the fund.

Mutual funds and their managers vary. From the macro level you essentially have two types of managers – active and passive. Active management means that the managers of the fund actively manage securities in hopes of achieving higher than market returns or outperforming their respective benchmark, commonly an index. Passive managers have more of a buy and hold mentality and will rarely trade unless it is necessary or if they are index fund managers and a specific company has been added to or removed from an index.

What active fund managers won't tell you is they will often play monkey see monkey do. Active fund managers may mimic what their counterparts are doing and buy and sell the same stocks or bonds. Rarely will you see a manager go out on a limb – there's too much to lose such as a well-paying job, or a sizeable bonus.

Studies have shown that many active managers will "hug" their respective benchmarks – meaning that rather than try to beat their benchmark by a wide margin, they will stay within a few percentage points, plus or minus to still meet their goals. An active manager that consistently beats the market by a wide margin will be expected to do the same year after year – a feat nearly impossible to do over the long run and in the short run, mostly due to luck.

Admittedly, there will be some managers that will beat the market. You'll see them announce their victories in financial publications showing stellar returns and how their fund beat the market.

Read the fine print.

In most cases they will be announcing their returns *before* expenses, called gross returns. Look at net returns, after expenses, and the same managers have now underperformed the market or their benchmark. And if they've been lucky enough to really beat the market by a wide margin, in most cases the next year the fund is scraping the bottom of the barrel.

In the long run your best bet is to simply buy and hold the market through passive management and index funds. Your expenses are less and you're not paying someone to do something they likely can't.

For more information on how active funds compare to their market benchmarks see:

https://us.spindices.com/spiva/#/

This website provides information regarding how difficult it is for active funds to beat their market benchmark.

Why Inactivity Can Be Your Best Friend

When most of us think about the word inactive, we may think negatively – such as lounging around on the couch, being lazy, or apathetic to a given situation. Most of us feel the need to be active to promote a healthy lifestyle through exercise, perform optimally at our job, or being involved with our family. In many cases, this is valid.

There is one area where inactivity can be beneficial. When it comes to investing, doing less can help us achieve the expected return we need on our portfolios, while keeping expenses as low as possible.

For many of us, this seems counterintuitive. Many of us can't help but to *do something*, anything. Some of us may feel that if we are in control of our investments, we can impact their performance.

But the truth is for most of us, we are not in control. We cannot control the markets. We cannot control the fluctuations. Being active in our portfolios to control volatility and returns is a frivolous endeavor.

What do I mean by active? Here are a few examples.

Selling out of a stock or fund when it is underperforming, without any other basis for consideration. Just because an asset is underperforming doesn't mean it should be sold. In fact, we should expect assets in our portfolios to underperform – to lose money from time to time. This means we are diversified.

Another example is buying an asset based on recent performance. Based on its recent good performance, we may feel it's bound to keep going up. We may also feel the need to buy and sell based off news reports, market prognosticators, or tips from family and friends. This can lead to the temptation of day trading – a recipe for disaster.

To paraphrase the great Warren Buffett, much can be attributed to inactivity, but investors cannot resist the urge to do *something*.

What do we mean by inactivity? Inactivity means once we have our asset allocation determined, and have the appropriate diversification among the asset classes, we need to sit back and let our investments do their work. This keeps expenses low, transaction costs to a bare minimum, and more importantly, allows us to focus on things we can control – such as other areas in our wealth management plan.

I jokingly call this a "Rip Van Winkle" portfolio. Set it up, fall asleep for many years, then wake up and look at how much money you have. We'll have saved money, time, and energy by not trying to control what we can't. And over time, we'll find that we've done way better in our investments than those who are busy (and stressing) for the sake of being active.

Good Market Years Can Be Deceiving

Good market runs are misleading. Too often, investors mistakenly think a top-performing year entitles them to refrain from putting away money the following year. These folks are cheating themselves.

True, the more return you get on your investments, the less you *must* save. What's false, though, is that your returns take the place of systematic saving for retirement, college, or just a rainy day. By no means reduce the amount you save while depending on the returns from bull years repeating or continuing upward.

Investment returns are the money you receive over a particular time frame – often largely theoretical money before you reach the age to withdraw from a retirement account penalty-free and without incurring capital gains taxes.

Let's say you invested in the S&P 500 or in an S&P 500 index fund and achieved almost 30% returns (not including dividends) for a given year. Not bad – but deceiving. That year was only one year.

If you save for retirement for 30 years, expecting 30% returns each year is like expecting your chickens to lay golden eggs.

What if you do stop systematically saving, thinking that a 30% increase in your portfolio offsets any additional money you didn't sock away? The result: disaster to your retirement plan.

Let's assume that two investors, Alex and Neil, are 30 and both plan to retire at 65. Both start with $10,000 in their IRAs at age 30 and both invest completely in the S&P 500. Up until the end of this year both also systematically contribute the annual maximum to their IRAs, now $6,500.

At the end of the year, both have $13,000 (from the 30% return) in their IRAs. Alex decides that since this year rocked, he won't contribute to his IRA again and instead believes that this year's return rates will last forever. Neil decides to keep steadily putting in his annual amount.

Neil is handsomely rewarded for his commitment. Over the next 35 years at a 6% average annual return (much more realistic historically), he amasses more than $768,000.

Alex saves sporadically, neglecting to contribute after up years in the market and contributing pell-mell after down years. Over the same span as Neil, he sees 20 years of down markets and 15 years of ups, investing his annual IRA maximum 20 times instead of Neil's 35.

To keep the math simple, let's say the market was down for the first 20 years, causing Alex to save, and then up the last 15 years, causing him to relax his savings commitment.

After the first 20 years, Alex has $133,000 assuming he suffers no losses in these down markets. For the next 15 years, Alex averages a 6% annual return and contributes nothing in these up years.

At the end of 35 years, Alex saves roughly $319,000 – or about $450,000 less than Neil.

Stick to your savings plan regardless of the market to take advantage of compounding returns and buying less in overpriced markets and more in underpriced ones.

The Power of Dollar Cost Averaging

If you're systematically saving for retirement through your 401(k) or with an IRA chances are you're taking advantage of dollar cost averaging.

Dollar cost averaging is a method of investing a specific dollar amount, generally monthly, no matter how the market is reacting. It's also a way for an investor to fully fund a retirement account without saving the maximum amount allowed in one shot.

For example, let's assume that an investor under the age of 50 wants to save to an IRA. The maximum contribution to the IRA for 2023 is $6,500. Should the investor want to save monthly, and still invest the maximum allowed for the year, she would simply divide by 12 and invest a sum of $500 monthly.

The beauty of this strategy is that the investor takes advantage of market swings, whether high or low. If the market is considerably high, the investor is buying fewer shares for the $500 invested. If the market falls, the investor (assuming he keeps investing – which he should) buys more shares for the same $500.

Over time, dollar cost averaging allows the investor to purchase shares for an overall lower cost per share. This strategy not only works for retirement savings, but also for college savings, or other investment goals. In fact, many individuals are already doing this via payroll deductions.

You're accomplishing a few things by dollar cost averaging. First, you're saving for retirement. Second, you're controlling emotions by investing consistently no matter what the market is doing.

Lastly, you're not trying to time the market. By dollar cost averaging you're *passively* timing the market by buying less when the market is high and more when it's low, all for the same monthly amount.

Let me explain why it's important to keep investing in a down market. I'm going to give an analogy that I think fits well. Imagine you want to purchase a flat screen TV. You've gone to the local store and find out that the TV you're looking for is $1,000. After waiting a week, you go back to the store to see that same TV has been marked down to $250, same TV, brand spanking new. Another week goes by and you see the TV is now priced at $1,250.

The question is: at which point do you buy?

Obviously, the answer is when the TV is priced at $250. You may consider buying four TVs since you planned on spending $1,000 anyway. Paying $1,250 is absurd, isn't it?

Many investors do the exact opposite when markets are rising or falling. Many individuals feel safety and security when the market is high and invest more.

Yet, those same individuals will not buy, and may even sell when the market is low or on sale, which is a recipe for disaster. This is a rare example where individuals feel better about paying more – for the same thing. It doesn't make sense.

Dollar cost averaging helps control this behavior. It systematically forces us to buy less when markets are high and possibly overpriced and more when they're on sale. Benjamin Graham, arguably the most famous investor and Warren Buffett's teacher, advocates dollar cost averaging in his seminal book, *The Intelligent Investor*. It helps take the emotion out of investing by passively forcing an investor to keep investing regardless of market volatility.

Can Watching The Market Make You Sick?

Feel like your health declines with each market low?

Here's why you may be right.

Two professors from the University of California at San Diego did a study that finds a correlation between market declines and admission rates to hospitals.

The authors claim that market dips affect your mental health almost instantaneously and add that expectations about the financial future play a role in today's happiness of you, the investor.

"Using individual patient records for every hospital in California from 1983 [to] 2011, we find a strong inverse link between daily stock returns and hospital admissions," write authors Joseph Engelberg and Christopher A. Parsons, "particularly for psychological conditions such as anxiety, panic disorder, or major depression."

This research benefits you on two fronts. It helps financial advisors educate you the client that, once you properly allocate assets, you gain little by logging into your account and watching the daily, even hourly, fluctuations of the market.

Every asset class fluctuates – which is why we diversify and allocate our money among real estate, stocks, commodities and bonds, to name a few. Any given time, any of these classes will be both in or out of favor. The more someone watches the gyrations, the more likely that person will reach for antacids or head to the hospital.

Second and self-evident: Not watching the market benefits your health and, I argue, your wealth. Unless you're a frantic day trader you have little need to look at your account more than once per month – less, if possible. Not watching the daily market movements lessens the chance you act on worry and succumb to the loser's game of trying to time and actively beat the market.

A down market can also spur you to stop investing in your individual retirement account, 401(k) or another savings plan. That's the *last* thing you want to do in a down market. In fact, consider investing more when the market drops.

Working with a professional financial advisor helps you control your emotions and think objectively in a market downturn. You still need to do homework: Make sure your advisor isn't in the same boat as you when markets fluctuate, becoming irrational and thinking emotionally.

Beware advisors who claim to be market prognosticators or who actively try to beat the market – almost an impossible feat and a goal most fund managers miss. Also, beware mere order takers – financial professionals who do whatever you ask as if you were ordering fast food from the drive-thru.

A good financial planner politely challenges your requests if he or she feels the idea goes against your best interest and wants to help prevent you from making a mistake hard to recover from. Think of all the sell orders placed in the 2008 crash, the worst move for investors at that time. Some folks' portfolios took irreversible damage.

To quote authors Daniel C. Goldie and Gordon S. Murray in *The Investment Answer*, "There are those that don't know, and those that don't know they don't know."

The market is much bigger than all of us. Don't worry about what you can't control. Maintain your financial health.

One of the Best Investments to Make

Traditionally when we think of investing our minds turn to stocks, bonds, mutual funds, or real estate. While these may or may not be the best investments for an individual's portfolio there is one investment that is almost always the right choice for anyone – human capital.

Human capital is an individual's worth of their own potential. Coined by economist Theodore Schultz, human capital can be invested like any other asset class to add value to an individual's life through earnings, health, and quality of life.

One of the classic examples of investing in human capital would be the decision to go to or go back to school. This enhances and expands an individual's knowledge of a subject or subjects and enables them to be more qualified for employment in that field. Such specialization (such as a doctor, attorney, professor, etc.) allows that individual to demand a higher income thus improving earnings, and (hopefully) quality of life.

However, carefully consider if the expense of such a degree or coursework will compound for you. What I mean is it's important to analyze whether the advance degree make sense financially. If the advanced degree will cost five to six figures, but return very little regarding financial increase, you may consider another route. While I am in favor of education, the last thing you should do is wind up six figures in debt without a significant financial return on that investment.

Another example of investment in human capital would be eating healthy foods and exercising. This allows for greater health which improves quality of life, longevity, and the potential to earn more as an individual is not decreasing their production due to missing work being sick. An individual may also save money by not paying higher life and health insurance premiums, medical bills, prescriptions, to name a few.

The good news is that investment in human capital doesn't have to be that costly. In other words, the returns can be exponential for very little cash outlay. For example, you may be able to check with your employer to see if they offer tuition assistance for you to take classes that will make you a more productive employee. Many employers do this as a benefit and it's not taxable to you (up to $5,250 in reimbursed expenses).

Several institutions offer online MOOCs (massive open online course) which are free online delivery of college course material, and other topics of study. Visiting different universities' web site can help guide you to the course that's relevant for you.

YouTube has an amazing selection of recorded material ranging from recorded finance classes from MIT to basic algebra from a community college. The Khan Academy also has a wide array of courses and material – all for free.

For your health, it doesn't cost a thing to put on some shoes and take a brisk walk or go for a run. Doing bodyweight exercises such as push-ups and pull-ups are free. Your employer may even offer discounts for joining the local health club. Eating healthy foods doesn't have to be expensive either. In fact, it may be less expensive to eat healthy – depending on what you're buying. The investment in your health and happiness boosts your human capital.

Finally, consider investing your time and resources to others. Your generosity and advice to others compounds in ways you may not see physically (such as monetary or other rewards) but it will reward you holistically and potentially spiritually.

After all, is anyone really self-made? I would argue no. They had help from others along their journey –

both seen and unseen. And with some luck, they were able to make the most of what they were given. You will too; and it will continue to compound.

Investing in your human capital with knowledge and health is an excellent addition to your (hopefully) well-diversified portfolio.

Chapter 5 – Retirement

How Retirement Plans Differ

Before you jump into a retirement plan at work, you need to know the rules for different types of accounts. Lots of investors think they know what a 401(k) is, but different types of workplaces have different types of accounts.

If you work for a hospital, say, your plan has some different features than does a 401(k), which is used at private companies. It is important to know how they differ and to discuss your choice with a financial professional before taking the plunge.

Let's start with the 401(k) because it is the most widely used and is a template for the others. This savings plan encourages both owners and employees to save for retirement. You can choose to have a specific dollar amount, or a percentage of your gross pay directed to your 401(k) account. You can invest in stock or bond mutual funds, individual stocks, your employer's stock (if you work for a publicly traded company) or even a money market account. Some employers permit people to invest in real estate and other less-liquid assets.

Your choice of funds depends on the company that offers the 401(k) through your employer. Generally, you should choose funds with low fees and expenses. As of 2023, the maximum amount you can put into your 401(k) is $22,500 annually plus another $6,500 if you're age 50 or older.

The 401(k) is tax-deferred, meaning that you don't pay taxes on the earnings now, but when you withdraw the money in retirement, the money is taxed as income. Withdrawals before age 59½ are subject to penalties (10%), with some exceptions. A cousin to the 401(k) is the 403(b). They are similar since you can invest a portion of your gross pay to your account, tax-deferred.

The 403(b) is for non-profits such as school districts, hospitals, municipalities and charitable organizations. Another difference is that, by law, the money in a 403(b) can only be invested in mutual funds or annuity contracts. You cannot own individual stocks or bonds in it. The yearly contribution limits and distribution rules are the same as for the 401(k).

The 457, a less common plan, is reserved for non-profits such as hospitals, government entities, school districts and colleges and universities. Many of the rules are the same as for the 401(k) and 403(b). The

457 only allows investments in mutual funds or annuity contracts.

Unlike the 401(k) and 403(b), the 457 lets you access your money at any age, if you leave your employer. For example, if you are 40 years old and saved $50,000 in a 457 and you lose or leave your job, you can use your 457 money without penalty. You simply pay ordinary income tax on any withdrawals.

Another key factor is the aggregation rule. What this means is that you can only invest $22,500 between a 401(k) and a 403(b). For example, let's say you work as a professor for nine months of the year and save $14,000 in your employer's 403(b). Over the summer, you work part-time for a company that offers a 401(k) plan and you want to save money there. Assuming you're under age 50, you can only save an additional $8,500 to your summer employer's 401(k) – for a total of $22,500.

The one exception to the aggregation rule is the 457. If you have access to all three types of plans, you can contribute the maximum to the 401(k) or 403(b), for a total of $22,500 – and then contribute the maximum $22,500 to the 457 for an annual total of $45,000. Of course, it isn't easy to sock away $45,000 per year, but it's an option.

Due to high administrative costs, a 401(k) plan is usually prohibitively expensive for smaller employers and self-employed workers – although solo 401(k)s have become more popular and less expensive to own.

Simplified Employee Pensions (SEPs) and Savings Incentive Match Plan for Employees (SIMPLE) individual retirement accounts are better solutions for these businesses.

For 2023, SEPs can be funded to a maximum of $66,000 or 25% of the employee's annual salary – whichever is smaller. One catch is that all employees must participate, so these are only suitable for small businesses with just a few employees.

With SIMPLEs, essentially both employer and employees participate, and the employer match employee contributions. As of 2023, you can contribute a maximum of $14,000 annually to a SIMPLE plan plus $3,000 if you're age 50 or older.

The aggregation rule that applies to the 401(k) and 403(b) also applies to SEPs and SIMPLEs. This means that of the four plans for 2023, you're still only allowed a total contribution of $22,500 annually ($29,000 if you're age 50 or over). Having a 457 is the only way to increase this amount.

Like SEPs and SIMPLEs, some companies match employee contributions in 401(k) and 403(b) plans up to a certain percent. You should take full advantage of this. It's basically free money. If you contribute $500 and your employer matches with the same amount, you already achieved a great return on your investment. Employers do this to comply with the plan requirements, and it also makes employees satisfied and loyal.

Finally, participating in your employer's plan does not stop you from funding a traditional or Roth IRA. You can contribute the maximum allowed by law to both your employer's plan and your own IRA. However, if your income is above certain amounts whether you file taxes single or married, you can no longer deduct the IRA contributions and you may no longer contribute to a Roth IRA.

It goes without saying that before you decide to participate, talk with your human resources department or a financial professional about which option or combination of retirement savings accounts is right for you.

Don't Leave Money on the Table!

Many individuals are offered an employer-sponsored savings plan though work such as a 401(k) or 403(b). Employers who offer these plans may provide a company match. This means that the employer will add money to the employee's account, if the employee saves a certain percentage of income. Some employers will even provide money even if the employee is not saving.

If you're employer offers a match on your contributions, take full advantage of it. Don't leave money on the table! This is free money – and it's unwise to not take it.

Let's look at an example.

Sam and Betty (both age 45) have a 401(k) and their employer offers a 50% match on employee contributions up to 5% of their salary. They both earn $80,000 annually. Sam decides to save 1% of his salary and Betty decides to save the maximum she can for 2023 of $22,500. Since the match is 5% of their salary, they both qualify for a maximum employer match of $2,000 (50% of 5% of $80,000).

Sam's contribution is $800, and his employer matches $400 for a total annual savings of $1,200.

Betty's contribution is $22,500, and her employer match is $2,000 for a total of $24,500. Sam has left $1,600 on the table. However, he's leaving a lot more than that over time.

Assume that Sam and better will work another 20 years to age 65. Let's also assume they invest in the same assets mix – a portfolio of 60% stocks and 40% bonds. Let's also assume a return of 5% over 20 years.

In 20 years, Sam has a sum of $39,679. Betty has nearly *twenty* times Sam's amount at $810,116. Granted, Betty saved more – she's smart. But what if Sam would have at least contributed to get the full employer match?

By saving 5% of his salary, Sam would have contributed $4,000, thereby qualifying him for the full employer match of $2,000 – saving a total of $6,500 annually. Over 20 years at 5% compounded Sam would have had $198,395. This is over $158,000 more than if Sam only saves 1% of his salary.

He left money on the table. A lot. We also assumed no raises, bonuses, etc. that would add to these amounts.

If you're saving to a Roth 401(k) or 403(b), the match from your employer will be added to a pre-tax account. As you may know, contributions to Roth accounts are made with after-tax money, and qualified withdrawals are tax-free. Employer matches made with pre-tax money will be taxed when withdrawn at your ordinary income tax rate.

This shouldn't discourage you from taking the full match. It's still free money. Think of it this way. Would you rather be taxed on zero money, or a pre-tax amount given to you for free from your employer – allowed to grow and compound over time?

And, the employer match is added on top of employee contributions. Recall Betty's scenario. Betty is maximizing her employee contributions this year at $22,500. Employer contributions are added to this amount. It's possible to save even more than the employee maximums each year if you have an employer match.

Finally, many employers have strings attached to their matches via vesting schedules. This means that for the match to be completely yours, you must work for your employer for a certain length of time. Common vesting schedules include 2 to 6-year graded vesting (where a portion of the match becomes yours over the 2 to 6-year time frame), or 3-year cliff vesting where all the match becomes yours after three years of employment.

Your employer match is free money. Don't leave any on the table.

Roth or Pre-Tax 401(k)?

At your job you likely have access to a 401(k). A 401(k) is an employer-sponsored (offered) retirement plan that allows you to save money for retirement. Sometimes your employer may provide a match based on a percentage of your contributions. *ALWAYS* take this match. It's free money. To not take it is foolish.

Your employer may give you the option of saving to a pre-tax account or a Roth account. A pre-tax contribution means that your contributions are made to your account before federal and state taxes are applied to your paycheck. A Roth contribution means that taxes are taken first, then the contribution goes to your account. This is also known as an after-tax contribution.

If you make pre-tax contributions, you avoid tax now, but you are then taxed when withdrawals are made – most likely in retirement. If you make Roth contributions now, you're taxed today, but withdrawals in retirement are tax-free. In both instances, your money grows tax-deferred.
It can make a lot of sense to contribute to your Roth 401(k)/403(b)/457(b) for a few reasons.

- If you're in a lower tax bracket now, you'll pay less tax on your contributions today, and avoid taxes in retirement when taxes rate may be higher, or your income is higher and taxed at a higher rate. This is especially true for young college graduates in their first job.

- The bulk of your money in your account will eventually be growth of your investments and reinvested dividends. With a Roth account, this will be tax-free when withdrawn at retirement.

- Having tax-free income in retirement means that your Social Security benefits may not be subject to taxation; since qualified Roth distributions are not taxable income.

- Mentally, not having to pay any (or very little) tax in retirement can be reassuring when it comes to planning for expenses, distributions, and bequeathing.

- It may mean that since your Roth distributions are not being taxed, any long-term capital gains (in a non-retirement account) may be subject to zero tax.

- You may not be able to make Roth IRA contributions (your income may be too high). A Roth 401(k) doesn't have income restrictions.

Personally, I favor Roth contributions. I like the tax-free benefit of qualified distributions in retirement. It should be noted however, that any employer match to a Roth 401(k) will be made to a pre-tax account (as the employer is allowed a tax deduction for the matching contribution). Your employer match will not be Roth dollars.

This should not be a discouragement from saving to your Roth 401(k).

Traditional or Roth IRA?

If you're thinking on starting and contributing to an IRA, you may be wondering which IRA is right for you. Generally, an individual has two IRAs to choose from – the traditional IRA and Roth IRA. In some cases, based on your income, the decision is already made. In all cases, to contribute to an IRA an individual must have earned income. This is generally W2 wages, Schedule C (self-employment) income, and income as an independent contractor (1099-MISC).

Let's start with the traditional IRA. For 2023, the maximum annual contribution amount is $6,500 for individuals under age 50. Those age 50 and over are allowed an additional $1,000 catch-up for a total of $7,000 annually. This is also true for Roth IRAs. Also, the annual maximums are the total among *all* IRAs. That is, if an individual is under age 50, they can have multiple IRAs, but the annual total among all of them cannot exceed $6,500 ($7,000 if age 50 or older).

Traditional IRA contributions may be tax deductible. For example, if an individual is not an active participant in an employer sponsored plan he or she is allowed a full deduction – regardless of AGI (adjusted gross income). However, if an individual is an active participant, then their deduction is subject to an AGI phase-out of between $73,000 - $83,000 if single and $116,000 - $136,000 if married filing jointly. If the individual is not an active participant but their spouse is, then the phase-out is $218,000 - $228,000. Any AGI above these phase-outs means deductibility of contributions is not allowed.

Traditional IRAs now allow contributions beyond the age of 73. Furthermore, traditional IRA owners must take required minimum distributions (RMDs) at age 73. Distributions may have different tax consequences depending on contributions made that were deductible or contributions made that were/are considered basis (after-tax contributions). Any taxable distributions are taxed as ordinary income. Generally, this will consist of any deductible contributions as well as any earnings on the growth.

The Roth IRA is a bit different. Although the contribution limits are the same as traditional IRAs, Roth IRAs also allow contributions after the age of 73 and do not have required minimum distributions for the account owner. Roth IRA contributions are never tax deductible. However, qualified distributions are received income tax free.

Additionally, individuals have access to their Roth IRA contributions at any time, without tax or penalty.

Roth IRAs are also limited to individuals with AGI below certain thresholds. For example, a single individual cannot contribute to a Roth IRA if their AGI is above $153,000 for 2023. Individuals who are married and file jointly cannot contribute to Roth IRAs if their AGI is above $228,000.

Both traditional and Roth IRAs have penalties for non-qualified distributions. The penalty is an additional 10% early withdrawal penalty in addition to ordinary income tax on earnings if there's a non-qualified distribution before age 59 ½. Some common exceptions to the 10% penalty (but do not avoid ordinary income tax) for IRAs include death, disability, expenses for higher education, and first-time home purchases up to $10,000.

If an individual is in a low tax bracket (such as a college graduate just starting out) a Roth IRA makes a lot of sense. The money contributed has been taxed at a lower rate and this allows the growth to be tax free in the future.

However, if an individual or couple earns too much, the Roth might not be an option – at least directly.

In this case, the traditional IRA is the only choice. From there, the individual needs to determine if they qualify for deductible contributions, or if they should consider a "backdoor Roth".

A "backdoor Roth" is where you can contribute after-tax money directly to a traditional IRA, and then immediately convert the amount to a Roth IRA. Specifically allowed by the Tax Cut and Jobs Act, this may be a strategy to consider if your AGI is too high to contribute directly to a Roth IRA.

The good news is that regardless of which IRA an individual owns, they can contribute to the IRA *and* their employer sponsored plan. For example, if an individual is under age 50 and is saving to a 401(k) and Roth IRA they can contribute the maximum of $22,500 to their 401(k) and the maximum of $6,500 to the Roth IRA – for a total of $29,000 per year!

Spousal IRAs

Many parents make the decision that after their child is born one parent will stay at home to be with the child. Some of the reasons include saving on daycare expenses and wanting at least one parent to bond and be with the child during those precious first few years of development.

Whatever the reason, the stay at home parent may leave a job and lose access to certain benefits – mainly their employer sponsored retirement savings plan. Although the stay at home parent has lost this benefit, it doesn't mean that they stop saving for retirement.

The stay at home parent can take advantage of the spousal IRA. Spousal IRAs aren't a specifically titled IRA. In other words, the IRA needn't be titled "Spousal IRA". It's simply an IRA in the stay at home parent's name - no different than if they had an IRA and were currently working, earning income.

To contribute to an IRA a person needs to have earned income. This means W2 wages from employment. Since the stay at home parent is not earning income, this may seem like an insurmountable obstacle. The solution however, is easy.

The stay-at-home parent can still contribute to a Traditional IRA or Roth IRA if the working spouse has enough earned income for the stay at home spouse to contribute. For example, let's assume that Mary is a stay at home parent and her husband Hank works a full-time job earning $60,000 per year.

For 2023, both Mary and Hank can make maximum IRA contributions of $6,500 to each of their IRAs (we're assuming they're under age 50). Hank can contribute from his earnings and Mary is allowed to contribute since Hank has enough earned income and Mary takes advantage of this as his spouse.

Although Mary may have lost access to her prior company's retirement plan, she can still save for her retirement if Hank has enough earned income. Finally, Hank and Mary's contributions are limited to Hank's earned income for the year. In other words, if Hank only had earned income of $8,000 for the year, he could put $6,500 in his IRA and only $1,500 in Mary's IRA for a total of $8,000 – his maximum earned income for the year.

Rolling Your 401(k) to an IRA

At some point, almost everyone changes jobs – often leaving behind retirement plans such as 401(k)s. Conventional wisdom holds that you roll that old employer-sponsored plan into a new individual retirement account. But what kind of new IRA?

First, you *can* roll your former employer's 401(k) into the plan from your new employer, which gets you continuing tax-deferred growth of your assets and deferred required minimum distributions, among other ongoing benefits. Not all employers accept rollovers from previous employers' plan, though, and investment options of your new 401(k) may be more limited in number compared with an IRA.

If you do decide to roll into an IRA, check:

Expenses. Generally, many employer-sponsored plans can offer investments (usually mutual funds) much cheaper than you as an individual can get in an IRA. Employers usually have many employees and plan providers have many clients in the same funds, leading to economies of scale.

Expense ratios, a measure of what it costs an investment company to operate your fund, therefore tend to be lower than in IRAs. Additionally, if you do roll over to an IRA, consider a fund company that doesn't charge loads (commissions to a broker, financial advisor or similar professional who selects holdings for the fund).

Funds flexibility. Some employer-sponsored plans offer funds with more congenial terms than you get with an IRA.

For example, an index fund in a 401(k) may allow you to contribute only $50 per period, where the same index fund outside of the plan might require a minimum $10,000 contribution. Some employer plans may offer mutual funds of companies not available to the general public, as well.

Taxes. Rolling over from a 401(k) to a traditional IRA is usually a non-issue when considering taxes. Rolling over from a pre-tax contribution plan such a 401(k) to a Roth IRA, on the other hand, almost certainly brings tax implications.

Your pre-tax money usually becomes taxable when this rollover (technically a Roth conversion) occurs. Your wisest move: Roll over the entire amount and pay the taxes from outside of the rollover amount.

If you want taxes withheld from the rollover amount, the Internal Revenue Service counts this withholding as a taxable distribution and, if you're younger than 59½, tacks on a 10% early withdrawal penalty.

Control. Generally, moving to an IRA gives you more control of your money than you had with a 401(k). You may also enjoy access to a broader selection of funds than in your old 401(k) and may also contribute more money to the IRA even after you left your employer.

Net unrealized appreciation (NUA). When you own your employer's stock in your 401(k), you can elect NUA tax treatment, meaning that the basis of the stock purchased is taxed as ordinary income and the stocks' subsequent appreciation incurs long-term capital gains tax rates. You lose NUA treatment if you roll over into an IRA.

The IRS has an excellent chart that shows which accounts you can roll money to and from. It can be found at:

https://www.irs.gov/pub/irs-tege/rollover_chart.pdf

Ask questions, seek advice, and talk to a competent, fiduciary financial planner about the details of your rollover.

Required Minimum Distributions (RMDs)

Generally, the earliest you can get access to money in your employer plan or IRA without being hit with a 10% penalty is 59 ½. However, participating in an employer-sponsored plan or traditional IRA means many individuals need to take required minimum distributions (RMDs) at age 73. RMD amounts are determined based on your age and your account balance – with an age factor (the number divided into your account balance) determined by the IRS.

In most cases, RMDs can be taken in an annual amount, or monthly via check or direct deposit. The specific RMD amount is based on the account balance as of December 31st the previous year and your age. Most custodians (where your money is invested) provide the amount that you must withdraw. You can also use an RMD calculator to get an idea of your RMD amount.

Additionally, be sure to account for any taxes you might owe. For 401(k) type plans, 20 percent will be automatically withheld for taxes. For IRAs, you must decide how much you want withheld, if any at all. Naturally, taxes don't apply to qualified Roth distributions.

However, RMDs are still required from Roth 401(k)/403(b)/457(b) plans. This is not the case for Roth IRAs – which do not have RMDs. To avoid RMDs from employer-sponsored Roth accounts, many individuals will do a qualified trustee-to-trustee transfer (rollover) from their employer-sponsored Roth account to their Roth IRA.

For those beginning their first RMDs, they have until April 1st the year following the year they turned 73 to take their RMD. While this delay is only allowed in this special circumstance, individuals need to be aware that if they choose to delay until April 1st of the following year, they'll need to take two RMDs in that year – one for the current year, and one for the previous year.

For example, Jim turns 73 in March of 2019. Jim can wait until April 1st, 2023 to take his 2019 RMD. However, since Jim waited until 2023 to take his 2019 distribution, he'll have to take his 2019 *and* 2023 distributions in the same year – 2023. This can have adverse tax consequences for Jim if he's taking taxable RMDs. Depending on the amount, it could put Jim in a higher tax bracket, increase his AGI, and lower his chances to qualify for other tax deductions or credits tied to AGI.

Finally, even though you must take an RMD, it doesn't mean you must spend it. You can reinvest the money, give to charity, or use the money to fund other opportunities – like college savings for grandchildren. Just remember, you cannot reinvest your RMD into a 401(k), IRA, or any other plan requiring "earned income" for contributions. RMDs are not considered earned income. However, the money can simply be invested in a non-qualified investment account or kept in a savings account.

Defined Benefit Pensions

A defined benefit pension is a type of retirement plan that your employer may offer as the only plan offered, or in conjunction with a 401(k) plan. If you have access to a defined benefit pension or are currently participating in one, you are in rare company as these types of plans are becoming few and far between.

Defined benefit pensions are different from 401(k)-type plans (called defined contribution plans) in several ways. One of the biggest differences is the fact that the employer is responsible for the funding of the plan in addition to accepting all the investment risk of the plan's assets. With a 401(k)-type plan, the employee is responsible for funding and the risk in the investment portfolio. Many defined benefit pensions are also backed by the Pension Benefit Guarantee Corporation (PBGC), which protects your pension up to a certain amount in event of plan termination.

Another difference is that at retirement, the defined benefit pension pays the retiree a guaranteed income stream for life (an annuity), and that guaranteed income may or may not have an inflation increase. If you're married, by law the pension must be paid as a joint and survivor annuity – meaning that if the spouse who has the pension dies, a benefit is still paid to the surviving spouse.

With a 401(k)-type plan, the account balance at retirement is based on the employee's contributions (and any employer match) and how it was invested. At retirement, the retiree is responsible for taking income from the account. They may choose to take periodic withdrawals, fund an annuity, or leave it invested should they not need the money just yet. The key point is the employee is responsible for these decisions. With a defined benefit plan, the decisions are already made, and if not, are very simplified.

The amount of the retirement benefit from a defined benefit pension is generally based on length of service, age, and final average salary. Thus, the longer you work and are participating in the pension, the higher the monthly benefit. Usually, companies will cap the years of service credit at some number such as 30 years – which means there's no increase in the pension based on working longer. Most companies allow employees to become "vested" (the pension is fully the employee's) after 5 years, sometimes less.

If you work for a company offering a defined benefit pension and are considering changing jobs, see if the new company has a defined benefit pension (among other benefits). Also check to see if you're vested in the current pension. If not, consider staying until you are. Even a small pension can make a difference in retirement. Naturally, this won't be your only criteria for staying or leaving but it's important.

Imagine receiving a guaranteed retirement income where no matter what happens, you'll get the same payment every month. Regardless of how the economy is doing, and regardless of your 401(k) or IRA performance, you'll get the same monthly amount. This is the beauty of a defined benefit pension.

Be Cautious of Pension Buyouts

If you're lucky enough to have a defined benefit pension, and even luckier if your employer still has it when you retire, you may find yourself in the position of having your employer offer you a pension buyout.

A pension buyout is when your employer offers you a lump sum at retirement (the present value of your total future pension payments), instead of you taking an annuity (a series of guaranteed monthly payments until you die).

Initially, this lump sum may look mouthwatering, as these lump sum amounts can be worth hundreds of thousands of dollars. However, before considering taking the buyout, it's important to understand what you're giving up in return, and the impact it may have on yours and your spouse's retirement.

Let's talk first about the benefits of a pension. As you may know, a pension is a guaranteed income stream paid to you (and your surviving spouse when you die) when you retire. In most cases, this is a legal obligation of your employer. Additionally, most pensions (except for governmental and a few others) are covered by the Pension Benefit Guarantee Corporation (PBGC). If your employer can no longer sustain the pension or goes bankrupt, the PBGC steps in to provide you with your pension, up to certain monthly limits.

As you can see, there's little risk to you when you take the guaranteed monthly pension payments. Funding, investment, and payment risk are all the responsibility of your employer and, if need be, the PBGC.

You have a guaranteed income stream for the rest of your life. If you qualify for Social Security (another form of guaranteed income), you may find yourself meeting most if not all your retirement expenses with these two income streams.

This is not the case if you take the lump sum. If you take the lump sum, your employer is effectively transferring all if the funding, investment, and payment risk to you – with no back up from the PBGC. Although the six-figure amount may look enticing, you've now accepted the fact that if it drops in value (due to investment volatility), that's your responsibility. How will it be invested – again, your responsibility. If you need the money to last yours and your spouse's lifetime, that's all on you.

Be very cautious and aware of the risks if your employer offers you a pension buyout. In most cases, this is a great deal for the employer but not ideal for you. Caveat emptor.

Annuities – Part I

You need a steady income flow in your retirement years and can build one with the right type of investment tool, such as annuities. The question is, what kind? One type has a fluctuating value that depends on market forces. Another type offers a steady payment. Here's a guide to figuring this out. Annuities grow through invested funds and then issue payments to you. When you contribute to an annuity you increase your number of accumulation units, which measures the value invested in the account. In effect, you buy shares of ownership of a large portfolio managed by the insurer.

During payout, in jargon terms, accumulation units become annuity units, a measurement of how much is available to pay to you. The number of annuity units remains the same for your lifetime. Annuities work well as another tool to back up your retirement funding and insure not outliving your money. Not every investor likes annuities, which lock your money for a set period of years. Early withdrawals also bring surrender charges that decrease over time.

Still, annuities defer taxes and offer some investors a comfortable balance between guaranteed investment and investing in the market.

Variable annuities allow you to contribute premiums and then allocate that money to different sub-accounts invested in various stock and bond mutual funds. One advantage: Sub-accounts allow you to easily change investment direction or allocation. The value of this type of annuity rises and falls with the fluctuations of the market and varies depending on what funds the portfolio manager invests the annuity in (stock mutual funds generally gyrate more than bond funds).

Variable annuities guarantee no constant amount at payout. The value likely changes depending on the value of the annuity units, according to current market conditions. They also work better if you want a portfolio to outpace inflation over time and you accept more investment risk to potentially achieve higher growth. In some states, annuities are even sheltered from creditors – a plus if you are sued. Many variable annuities shield you against market losses with a guaranteed minimum income benefit (GMIB) that ensures you receive a minimum value's worth of payments. GMIBs tend to come with hefty fees and lots of strings attached.

Fixed annuities pay a fixed interest rate and are often guaranteed and generally more conservative. They fluctuate less than a variable annuity and, on the other hand, may not keep pace with inflation depending on the interest rate guaranteed in the contract. They work best if you want a guaranteed rate and accept slow, steady growth.

Cons of fixed annuities include lack of liquidity and flexibility once you buy one – locking up assets you might instead want to leave to heirs. The annuity account also pays out whatever it's worth at your death.

Annuities – Part II

We covered some of the differences in annuities and the various types of annuities you can purchase. Now I want to explain some of the fees and expenses that some annuities and annuity providers employ. Then we'll look at how annuities are taxed.

As mentioned previously, annuities are an insurance product – insuring against longevity. Most companies that offer annuities will charge for this insurance by means of what are called mortality and expense charges. M&E charges can be as low as .25% to as high as over 2%. These charges are the expenses the annuity company charges to the entire risk pool of policyholders to pay for the few that will outlive their life expectancy. Most policyholders and annuitants will not outlive their life expectancy and thus pay for those that do.

M&E charges will also help the annuity company cover other administrative expenses and a contingency for profits.

For example, let's say you own a fixed annuity that pays 3% guaranteed interest, but the M&E charges are 1.25%. Your net return for any given year is really 1.75%, not 3%.

Most annuities will also have significant surrender charges. Surrender charges are charges the policyholder pays if they cancel their contract early – usually within 6 to 10 years. Most of this charge is to cover the commission paid to the person selling the annuity and the insurance company must recover that commission from somewhere – and it's usually from the policy holder. Surrender charges can be as high as 10% and gradually decline by percentage the longer you own the annuity.

Variable annuities will have additional expenses in the form of expense ratios for the mutual funds that hold the policyholder's money. Expenses can be as low as .25% to as high as 2.5%. Generally, expense ratios will be high if you're invested in a fund that the insurance company owns. It's their proprietary mutual fund and they are the usually worst to have money in.

All it takes is some simple math to realize that on average fees and expenses can be as low as .50% to as high as 4%. Some annuities will be even higher if there are added riders and benefits to the policy such as guaranteed income riders, guaranteed minimum withdrawal benefits, or guaranteed interest options. But there's no free lunch. Usually the more bells and whistles you have, the more expensive the annuity and the *less* return you get.

For example, if you had a variable annuity that returned 6% in a given year, if your total expenses were 4% - you only made 2%. Most of the fees and expenses are going to be buried in the prospectus (a several hundred-page book), but it will disclose the total fees as well as the surrender charges.

A few words of caution: Beware of having an IRA with an annuity wrapper. This is overkill. Why? Annuities are tax deferred vehicles – meaning that money that accumulates inside the annuity is not taxed until it's withdrawn. The same is true with IRAs. You don't need both to get the tax-deferral. And be extremely cautious of having a Roth IRA within an annuity.

From a tax perspective, annuities are taxed on a last in first out basis – meaning earnings and growth are taxed first. An annuity in a 401(k), 403(b), or 457(b) plan will be taxed entirely as ordinary income. One exception is when someone chooses to annuitize a lump sum such as an after-tax amount of money or a life insurance death benefit.

This taxation is calculated using the exclusion ratio. For example, let's say you have $500,000 that you want to use to guarantee yourself a lifetime income stream. The insurance company says that based on your life expectancy you will live for another 20 years and will get $4,000 per month from your $500,000 initial deposit. Since $500,000 of your initial investment has already been taxed, part of the payment you receive will not be taxed.

The calculation works like this:

$500,000/($4,000 x 12) x 20 years; or $500,000/$960,000. This means that 52% of the $4,000 payment ($2,080) is not subject to income tax. The remaining $1,920 is taxable. This ratio will remain if the annuitant is within his or her life expectancy. Should he or she live beyond 20 years, then all the $4,000 is taxable since the $500,000 basis is exhausted.

It goes without saying that if you're considering an annuity or being *pressured* to buy an annuity, seek a second opinion. Be sure to ask about the annuity's total cost including M&E charges, expense ratios (if a variable annuity), and the surrender charges. Also consider asking the salesperson how much they'll make on the sale. If they don't know the charges or commissions – this is a bad sign. Consider looking elsewhere.

Ask yourself if you really *need* an annuity. If a pension, Social Security, and your other retirement account balances will cover your living and retirement expenses, then an annuity may not be in your best interest. If you don't have a pension, and your Social Security and retirement income may not be enough, then an annuity may be an option.

Finally, annuities are not bad. They can be an excellent hedge against outlasting your income. But they can also destroy an investor's returns via fees and expenses. Ask lots of questions and seek the advice of a competent professional – someone whose income is not contingent on the sale of the annuity.

Guaranteed Income (Annuitization)

Annuities sometimes get a bad rap. The distaste people have for annuities may be based on a bad experience with a salesperson, the fear of "the insurance company getting all your money when you die", or just plain misinformation.

Annuities can be a great choice for your retirement. That is, after annuitization an annuity provides a guaranteed income stream to you and or your spouse for the rest of your lives. Think of this as your own defined benefit pension. In fact, if you don't have a defined benefit pension, you may consider the guaranteed income a private annuity provides. The guarantee comes from the insurance company providing the annuity. To date, no insurance company as ever defaulted on its annuity obligations.

So why can annuitization be a good thing for you?

Let's look at an example.

Let's say you've determined when you retire that your annual expenses are $115,000. This sum includes your living expenses, taxes, and doing fun things in retirement (such as travel, dining out, and hobbies). You've determined that Social Security will provide $30,000 per year which leaves $85,000 to be covered with other retirement savings.

It's safe to say that Social Security is providing $30,000 (inflation adjusted) per year in guaranteed income. In other words, you know that at the very least you'll always have $30,000 per year for income, or $30,000 of expenses will always be covered. But maybe you're uncomfortable with knowing only $30,000 is guaranteed. This is where the annuity can help.

Depending on the amount of money you have saved for retirement, you could purchase an annuity to provide a guaranteed income stream that meets 50, 75, or even 100 percent of your needed income – for the rest of your life! The amount you choose to annuitize will be dependent on several factors such as retirement savings, other income, RMDs, and estate goals (gifts and inheritances).

The flip side, however, is what can happen if you die before your life expectancy. It is true that in some circumstances the insurance company keeps your money (if you had a single life annuity) and this money goes back into the risk pool of other annuitants. But there are options to make sure that this doesn't happen such as joint and survivor annuities, period certain annuities, and refund annuities. Discussion of these options is beyond the scope of this book.

Annuitizing a portion of your retirement income shouldn't be readily dismissed. Guaranteeing some of your income can reduce stress, meet certain retirement expenses, and ensure you never run out of money. Should you need help navigating your options, consider working with a fiduciary – preferably one who doesn't sell annuities.

Social Security – The Basics

The following provides some of the basics of Social Security. Concepts such as filing strategies, GPO, WEP, and others are beyond the scope of this book. For a deeper dive into Social Security, I recommend Jim Blankenship's book, *A Social Security Owner's Manual.*

When you achieve your full retirement age (FRA) under Social Security, you become eligible to receive 100% of your primary insurance amount (PIA). Your FRA is determined by the Social Security Administration and is likely between 66 and 67 years of age. Your PIA is determined by how long you've worked, and your wages earned during your working lifetime.

Whether you're young and working or nearing retirement age, it's important to understand how this *guaranteed* retirement benefit works, and how it can work for you.

The earliest you can take your retirement benefit is age 62. The latest you can wait to take your benefit is age 70. Taking your benefit before FRA or delaying your benefit after FRA will have an impact on the monthly amount you ultimately receive. Taking an early benefit reduces your monthly amount while delaying your benefit increases it.

If you take your benefit early, your benefit is reduced by 5/9 of 1% per month for the first 36 months you take your benefit before FRA. For any months beyond the first 3 years, your benefit is reduced by 5/12 of 1% per month for up to 24 months.
If you delay taking your benefit, your benefit is increased by 2/3 of 1% per month, or 8% annually, up to age 70. There is no increase in benefit for delaying after age 70. Both the reduction and increase calculations are based off your PIA.

For example, let's say your PIA at FRA (lots of acronyms here) is $1,000. We'll assume your FRA is age 67. If you take your benefit at age 62, that's 5 years or 60 months total. The first 36 months will use the 5/9 calculation. Thus, 36 multiplied by 5/9 is a 20% reduction.

Next, since there are 24 months remaining, we multiply 24 by 5/12 which is a 10% reduction. The two percentages are added together for a total reduction of 30%. Instead of $1,000, you'd receive $700 at age 62.

If you took your benefit at age 65, then only the 5/9 calculation is used since it's always applied on the first 36 months of taking benefits early.

Assuming you delayed your benefit until age 70, then your PIA is increased by 8% annually (2/3 of 1% monthly). In our example, your benefit is increased a total of 24% (8% multiplied by 3 years) for a total delayed benefit of $1,240 – an increase of $240 per month! Delaying even one year increases your benefit by 8% - or $80 monthly in our example.

The decision of when to take your benefit should not be made lightly. A lot can factor into it such as your longevity, spousal benefits, survivor benefits, etc. Discussing your benefit options with the Social Security administration as well as a financial professional can help you navigate these waters.

Reverse Mortgages

As you near retirement, you may foresee a need for more money in the golden years than your savings can handle. You look to use Social Security, careful withdrawals from qualified accounts and maybe annuities. You can also use one of your biggest assets: your home and its equity in the form of a reverse mortgage.

With a second mortgage, or a home equity line of credit, you must make monthly payments on the principal and interest. In a reverse mortgage, you use the equity in your home to receive monthly income payments. Generally, once you die or sell the home, you or your survivors use the remaining equity to pay off the loan.

You must live in the home as a primary residence – no renting it out – for the life of the loan. There's also a limit on the amount you can borrow from such sources as the U.S. Department of Housing and Urban Development (HUD). Among other conditions:

- Lenders generally charge an origination fee and other closing costs, as well as servicing fees over the life of the mortgage. Some also charge mortgage insurance premiums.

- You can't deduct interest on your reverse mortgage on your income tax returns.

- You remain responsible for property taxes, insurance, utilities, fuel, maintenance and other home expenses. Fail to keep any of these up and the lender might require you to repay your loan.

- A financial assessment is required when you apply. Your lender may require a set-aside amount to pay your taxes and insurance during the loan. The set-aside reduces the amount of funds you can get in payments.

- Reverse mortgages can use up the equity in your home, which means fewer assets for you and your heirs.

One popular form of a reverse mortgage is HUD's home equity conversion mortgage (HECM). To qualify, you must be 62 or older, live in a single-family home or a 2-to-4-unit home where you occupy one unit (HUD-approved condominiums and some manufactured are also eligible) and receive advice from a HECM-approved counselor who educates you on the advantages and disadvantages of such a mortgage.

With a HECM, you also still own your home. HECM loans are non-recourse, meaning you'll never owe more than the value of your home at its sale regardless of whether the home's value declines.

Other types, according to the U.S. Federal Trade Commission (FTC):

Single-purpose reverse mortgages are often a least-expensive option, offered through some (not all) state and local government agencies, as well as nonprofit organizations. You use these loans for only one purpose, which the lender specifies (for example, home repairs, improvements or property taxes).

Proprietary reverse mortgages are private loans backed through lending companies. If you own a higher-valued home, you may get a bigger loan advance.

Shop around carefully for a good reverse mortgage for you, the FTC recommends:

- Compare fees and costs. While the mortgage insurance premium is usually the same lender to lender, most loan costs – including origination fees, interest rates, closing costs and servicing fees – vary.

- Understand total costs and loan repayment. Ask a counselor or lender to explain the total annual loan cost (TALC) rates, which show your projected annual average cost of a reverse mortgage, including all the itemized costs.

- No matter what type of reverse mortgage you consider, understand all the reasons you might have to repay your loan before you planned.

When you sell or convey title of the property, die or do not maintain the property as principal residence for longer than 12 months due to physical or mental illness, you reach what's called the maturity event, meaning your reverse mortgage becomes due and payable.

Nevertheless, when you do the deal right a reverse mortgage can increase your chances of a healthy income in your golden years, especially if you use the money in conjunction with other income such as Social Security, pensions, annuities, and payouts from your retirement accounts.

An Emergency Fund for Retirement

Earlier in this book we discussed having an emergency fund while working and saving for retirement. The rule of thumb has been to keep 3 to 6 months of non-discretionary living expenses on hand in case one loses their job, becomes disabled, or an unforeseen emergency occurs. But what about those individuals who are already retired? What should their emergency fund look like? Do they even need one?

One of the bigger risks that retirees face in retirement is sequence risk. Sequence risk is generally defined as the risk of even lower portfolio returns due to making withdrawals from a retirement account when the market has experienced a downturn.

In other words, a retiree experiences sequence risk when their IRA (or other retirement plan) drops in value due to market volatility, and they make a withdrawal (or withdrawals) after the account has dropped in value. Another way to put it would be like an individual saving for retirement in their 30s yet selling at the market bottom and "locking in" their losses.

Understandably, this can be disastrous for any retiree who has a goal of their money outlasting them in retirement. There are a few things pre-retirees and retirees may consider helping reduce sequence risk.

- Consider having 1-2 years of living expenses in a savings account. This can help reduce the strain on the retirement account when markets are down by living off the money in the "emergency fund" for retirement. Additionally, an individual may consider funding the emergency savings with money from the retirement account when markets are up in any given year. That is, sell from the asset classes that are up to replenish the cash account.

- Consider longevity insurance (an annuity). By purchasing longevity insurance an individual can transfer some of the sequence risk to the insurance company providing the annuity. If their non-annuitized portfolio drops in value due to market volatility, the individual can take some comfort in knowing they will not have to withdraw as much from their assets since they will be receiving a guaranteed income stream from the annuity.

- Consider reducing spending temporarily. If possible, the individual can delay consumption until their portfolio improves. Granted, not everyone can afford to reduce spending (such as for health care, housing, etc.), but some individuals may find it to their advantage to delay the vacation, not dine out as much, or delaying discretionary purchases until their financial picture improves.

- Optimize your Social Security. There are many advantages and nuances an individual or couple can consider when applying for and taking Social Security benefits. By taking advantage of the options available, individuals may be able to maximize their income from Social Security (essentially an annuity) and help provide more guaranteed income during volatile market times.

Don't Dismiss That "Small" Pension

Frequently, I'll meet with clients to go over a retirement plan. As is typical, we look at current investments, account balances, Social Security, etc.

Often these conversations revolve around distributions from retirement plans, taxes, and cash flow planning to reduce the probability of portfolio failure and ensuring an income stream that is congruent with the clients' retirement goals.

Sometimes clients will also have small pensions from their current or former employer and they will tell me that they are small, trivial, or not worth considering.

Whenever I hear those words, I try to explain to the clients that however small or trivial, it's still a guaranteed income stream that will last the rest of their lives in many cases.

For example, I have seen clients think that a $150 monthly pension wasn't a big deal. But when I present to them that it's an amount for a "date night" once a month, they can visualize using that money for the date night. A similar expense would be cable TV, funding a grandchild's 529 plan, etc.

In another example, some clients had roughly $350 in monthly pension money coming from two different sources. They were concerned about having a travel fund in retirement. Their travel budget in retirement was approximately $8,000. When I mentioned they could allocate the pension money to fund half of their annual travel budget, they could visualize the pension money being used, and were almost relieved that they didn't have to worry about where (half) of their travel budget would come from.

In other words, half of their travel budget was guaranteed by the "small" pension money that was almost an afterthought of our conversation.

The point is, with a pension, that amount can be allocated to cover a specific retirement expense and individuals can know that a certain expense or expenses are going to be met by the pension. It means one less expense to worry about where the money is going to come from, and it can reduce stress knowing that no matter what, the client is always guaranteed to meet that expense.

Put another way, per the examples above, you can guarantee you will have a travel fund, fund a grandchild's education, or a monthly date night in retirement.

Can I Retire Early?

Many individuals at some point in their life and career wonder if they can retire early. Retiring early is relative to the individual. Retiring early for one person may mean retiring at age 55. To another, it may mean retiring at age 30.

When teaching, I'll ask my students what the "retirement age" is. Answers usually range from 65 to 70. When I tell them it's whatever age they choose, you can see the metaphorical wheels turning. Inevitably, I will get asked the question, "How much money do you need to retire?" And the answer is the crux of this piece.

Whether an individual wants to retire can be based on several factors such as money saved, age, job satisfaction, and health. For example, an individual may never want to "retire" if they love their job, or if they find fulfilment and purpose while at work.

For some individuals, the choice to retire isn't a choice. They must continue to work to cover expenses, health care, etc. Perhaps they never saved for retirement. Sometimes these individuals work until they physically cannot do so any longer. Maybe their only retirement income is Social Security.

Back to the crux. The answer I tell my students (and clients) is that how much you need to retire is a function of how much you need to spend in retirement. For example, I have seen clients needing only $38,000 annually to cover expenses and live comfortably in retirement, and half of that amount was covered by Social Security. This meant the clients only needed to cover $19,000 of annual expenses from their retirement portfolio. Based on their portfolio, they had more than enough. In another scenario, the clients' need hovered around $250,000 annually. Sadly, their portfolio would last less than 13 years.

In other words, you may be comfortable retiring with $500,000 saved, or you may find $5,000,000 will not be enough.

To retire "early" is relative to what early means for you and how much money you feel you would need to live on in retirement. For young individuals reading this article, it means saving a lot of money while they're young, to reap the benefits of not working later, should you choose. For older individuals, it may mean saving much more (if they didn't start saving early), and perhaps cutting expenses to achieve their retirement goal. And still for others, it may mean continuing to work, since they love what they do and have no intentions to retire.

The choice is yours.

Chapter 6 – Tax

Taxation of Income, Capital Gains, and Interest

When you receive income, it's likely going to be subject to taxation. However, the *type* of income will determine the specific tax treatment, and ultimately determine how much you get to keep.

We can break income down into three basic types: ordinary income, capital gains income, and interest income. Here's a breakdown of each.

- Ordinary Income – Ordinary income (OI) is income received that is subject to ordinary income tax rates. These tax rates are the rates individuals pay on incremental amounts of income. Rates can be as low as 10% and as high as 37%. Income typically subject to OI rates is income from your wages (W2, self-employment), taxable bond interest, taxable retirement income, and annuity income.

- Capital Gains Income – Capital gains income occurs from the sale of assets such as stocks, bonds, mutual funds, ETFs, real estate*, and other assets. Depending on how long the assets were held determines if capital gains are taxed at OI rates or more favorable long-term rates. Assets held for one year or less and then sold, have any gain subject to OI rates. Asset held longer than one year and then sold have gains taxed at long term capital gains (LTCG) rates – which are either 0%, 15%, or 20% - depending on your total income. The higher your total income, the higher the LTCG rate you'll pay. Qualified dividends from stocks are generally taxed at the favorable LTCG rates.

- Interest Income – Interest income is income from assets that generate interest such as bonds, savings accounts, CDs, treasuries (savings bonds, T-bills, etc.), and money market accounts. In most cases this income is taxed at OI rates. One exception is interest from municipal bonds issued by city or state governments. Interest on these bonds is not taxable at the federal level and may avoid state and local taxation as well.

Knowing how specific income is taxed can help with the process of where to hold specific assets and in which accounts – called asset location (discussed later). This can improve your tax efficiency. Additionally, capital losses (selling an asset for less than you paid for it) may be used to offset other income, also improving tax efficiency.

These are the basics of income. Naturally, there are going to be exceptions and complexities that may apply to you. To avoid costly mistakes, you may benefit from the advice of a tax professional -usually a CPA who specializes in tax, an Enrolled Agent (EA - enrolled to represent taxpayers before the IRS), or a tax attorney.

*Gains on the sale of your primary residence may not be taxed up to $250,000 for single and up to $500,000 for married tax filers. Specific rules apply.

Credits and Deductions

Let's talk a little bit about tax credits and tax deductions. Both can be used to help reduce or avoid taxation but behave differently when it comes to doing so.

Tax deductions are beneficial because they help lower the amount of your income subject to taxation. Deductions may be either "above the line" or for AGI, or "below the line" or from AGI. The line in the sand in this scenario is of course, AGI (adjusted gross income).

Above the line deductions are beneficial because they reduce gross income to arrive at AGI. A lower AGI may result in being able to take advantages of other benefits in the Internal Revenue Code (IRC) such as being able to contribute to a Roth IRA and qualifying for additional tax credits (discussed below).

Common above the line deductions include student loan interest, deductible contributions to a traditional IRA, and self-employed business expenses (Schedule C).

Once AGI is reached, below the line deductions can be applied. Below the line deductions lower AGI further, to arrive at taxable income. Below the line deductions are going to come from either itemized deductions (Schedule A) or the standard deduction — a deduction everyone qualifies for and varies in amount based on filing status. You may either itemize or take the standard deduction, but you cannot do both.

If you itemize, you'll use Schedule A. Common deductions on Schedule A include medical and dental expenses, home mortgage interest, state and local taxes, and charitable contributions. Some deductions on Schedule A (such as medical and dental) are subject to a floor of AGI. An AGI floor means that the expenses may be deducted once they're higher than the floor. For example, if your AGI is $100,000 and the deduction has a floor of 10%, then any expenses *above* $10,000 would be deductible.

Once all deductions have been taken, you arrive at your taxable income. It's here where the applicable tax rates are applied, and your tax is calculated. However, you may still benefit from tax credits.

Tax credits reduce the amount of tax owed on a dollar-for-dollar basis. Whereas deductions reduce taxable income, credits lower the amount of taxed owed. For example, if you owe $2,000 in taxes but have $1,500 worth of credits, then your net tax owed would be $500. In some instances, your tax credits may eliminate any tax owed. In fact, you may even qualify for a refund based on your credits exceeding the tax you owe (called refundable or partially refundable credits).

Naturally, the specific credit(s) you may qualify for depends on your situation. For example, parents can take advantage of the child tax credit, American opportunity tax credit, child and dependent care credit, and the earned income tax credit. Other credits you may be eligible for are the lifetime learning credit, saver's credit, adoption credit, and residential energy credit.

To see what credits and deductions make the most sense for your situation, talk to a tax professional such as a CPA that specializes in taxes, an EA, or tax attorney. You don't want to leave money on the table or pay more tax than required.

Lowering Your Taxes (Legally)

When tax time approaches, you may find yourself gathering all of last year's tax information and getting ready to file your income taxes. Maybe you expect a refund or maybe you dread writing a check to Uncle Sam. If the latter, here are some tips to reduce your tax burden.

Contribute more to your 401(k). You make these contributions in your retirement plan *before* you pay tax on the money. This lowers the amount of your taxable income, potentially reducing the amount you may owe at tax time and increasing your retirement savings.

Contribute enough of a percentage of your pay to get your employer match. Many employers match around 5% of an employee's pay.

Take advantage of a deductible individual retirement account contribution. If your employer doesn't offer a plan, set up and automatically save post-tax dollars to an individual retirement account. Your contributions to a traditional IRA may be tax-deductible; withdrawals from a Roth IRA in your retirement will be tax-free.

Generally, your deduction for the above IRAs may drop or completely disappear if you already have a workplace 401(k) available and your income exceeds certain limits.

Increase withholding. Changing the amount withheld from your paycheck can help you decrease, if not eliminate, what you owe at tax time. An IRS calculator helps you figure how much to withhold and how much of your paycheck to keep.

Events during the year may also change your marital status or the exemptions, adjustments, deductions or credits you expect to claim on your tax return. You may need to give your employer a new IRS Form W-4 to change your withholding status or number of allowances.

Make your home energy-efficient. Investing in lowering your home's energy consumption may open up credits to in turn lower your overall tax bill.

Improvements qualifying for credits include devices to harness solar and wind energy, geothermal heat pumps and electricity-producing fuel cells. These credits often cover almost a third of the cost of installation. You can also credit up to $500 for more usual improvements such as insulation, exterior doors and windows and heating and cooling equipment.

Start or increase your charitable giving. Giving to help others not only feels good – the IRS also provides some tax breaks for charitable givers. From giving to your church to donating items to the local foundation, you can open your heart *and* lower your tax bill.

These breaks do come with conditions:

- You can't deduct contributions to specific individuals, political organizations and candidates, and you must give to a qualified organization. See IRS Publication 526, "Charitable Contributions," for what constitutes such an organization and for income limits to claim deductions.

- To deduct a charitable contribution, you must file IRS Form 1040 when you file your taxes, and you must itemize deductions on Schedule A.

- If you receive a benefit because of your contribution such as merchandise, event tickets or other goods and services, you can deduct only the amount that exceeds the fair market value of the benefit.

5 Tax Credits You Don't Want to Miss

As you file your tax returns there are some tax credits that you may qualify for to help reduce, if not eliminate your tax liability. The credits below are common, but not exhaustive of all credits available. Talk with your tax professional to see which credits you qualify for. Additionally, most of these credits are subject to AGI phaseouts – meaning they can be reduced or eliminated the higher your AGI.

- Child Tax Credit. This credit may be worth up to $2,000 per child, depending on income. The child must be under age 17 at the end of the year, as well as be a dependent and a US citizen.

- The American Opportunity Tax Credit. This tax credit for education expenses is allowed for parents for up to the first four years of post-secondary (college) education. The benefit of this credit is that it is a "per student" credit. This means the credit can be taken for multiple children in college. The maximum credit per student is $2,500.

- The Lifetime Learning Credit. Like the AOTC, this credit can be claimed for education expenses. The difference between this credit and the AOTC is that this credit is a "per family" credit. This means the maximum amount of $2,000 allowed is in total regardless of how many family members are in college. However, this credit can be used for an unlimited number of years in college.

- The Saver's Credit. This credit allows taxpayers with lower incomes a credit of $1,000 (single) or $2,000 (MFJ) who are saving for retirement. This credit helps individuals by allowing them to take a credit based off of money contributed to retirement accounts such as a 401(k) or IRA. This credit is also called the retirement savings contributions credit.

- Child and Dependent Care Credit. This credit can be taken by individuals who pay for child care expenses in order to work or are active seeking work. The credit cannot exceed $3,000 for one qualifying individual or $6,500 for two or more individuals.

A Quick Trick to Reduce Your Tax Liability

Perhaps you've paid an excessive amount of tax to Uncle Sam and are looking for ways to reduce your tax liability for next year.

Let's say that you and your spouse both work and file your taxes jointly. Your tax liability for this year was $4,000 – meaning that's the amount of the check you wrote to the IRS. Now you're looking for a potential way to reduce that liability – at least in the here and now. Let's assume your marginal tax rate is 22%.

The quick trick in this example is to take your tax rate which is 22% and divide it into your tax liability of $4,000. In this case it turns out to be nearly $18,200. This magic number of $18,200 is what you or your spouse could contribute to your pre-tax retirement plan such as a 401(k), etc.

All else being equal, this significantly reduces your tax liability for the year. The reason why is that the money deferred to your retirement accounts is taken from your paychecks before taxes are taken out, thus you have less money that's subject to taxation. And in this case – you're paying yourself first!

Granted, you will eventually have to pay tax on the amounts in your retirement plans, but what you're doing now is reducing your tax liability in the present and paying for it later. This may work out for you as your tax rate in the future may be lower than your current 22%. It could also work against you if your tax liability happens to be higher when you start taking money from your retirement accounts.

State Taxes & Retirement

If you live in a state that doesn't tax retirement income, you save on taxes if you fund your 401(k) or other employer-sponsored plan instead of a Roth individual retirement account. If you plan on relocating when you quit working, look at how your new home state treats retiree income.

The advantage of the Roth is that it offers tax-free distributions. You pay state and federal tax today, but you don't have to worry about it when you take distributions during retirement. Here in Illinois, where I live, and several other states, the current law exempts retirement income from state taxes.

Any contributions to a 401(k), 403(b), SEP, SIMPLE or 457 avoid state income taxation. Qualified distributions at retirement are only taxed at the federal level, and then only as income.

If you contribute directly to a Roth IRA, you pay tax on that money before it goes in. It's taxed at both the federal and state level. At retirement, your 401(k) distributions are state tax-free. The state never touches your 401(k) money, whether going into the plan or taken out when out retire. The Roth, funded with your after-tax dollars, doesn't enjoy such an advantage.

State's treatment of retirement income should figure into your decision of where to live when you retire. In addition to Illinois, Mississippi, and Pennsylvania don't tax income from retirement account contributions. Alaska, Florida, Nevada, South Dakota, Texas, Washington, and Wyoming don't have any income tax at all, so your 401(k) and non-Roth distributions are not taxed there either.

The states that do tax retirement income, or even Social Security, often have income and age limits. Of course, there are other state or local levies, such as on property and on retail purchases, that you should note as well.

If you live in the retirement-tax-friendly states, you can avoid paying extra taxes if you contribute to your employer's plan and then at retirement or whenever you leave your job, convert that money to a Roth IRA. In this case the money is already deferred from state taxation and then, when it's converted to a Roth IRA, avoids state income taxation again since it is income from a retirement plan, which the state does not tax.

Another way to avoid this is if your employer's plan allows, convert your 401(k) to a Roth 401(k) while you're still employed. Again, you pay federal income tax but avoid the state taxation if your state excludes retirement income. If you're in a higher tax bracket, it's a good idea to convert small amounts over many years to avoid bumping yourself into an even higher bracket with a huge one-time conversion. Or you may just want to wait to convert the whole amount when you know you move into a lower tax bracket.

If you live in California or another state that doesn't exclude retirement income from taxes, the only way to avoid paying taxes on your distributions is to defer money to a Roth IRA. It gives you tax-free retirement income and shields you from potential increases in your tax rate.

Unless your gross income excludes you from contributing directly to a Roth IRA, you are currently at a very high tax rate and expect it to go down in the future, or you live in one of the retiree-friendly states mentioned above, the Roth IRA is the best way to go.

Asset Location

Diversification and asset allocation are important components to any investment plan. Additionally, in which accounts assets such as stocks and bonds are held, also called asset location, should be considered.

Asset location refers to the type of account that assets are held. Such accounts are generally traditional and Roth IRAs, employer-sponsored plans such as 401(k)s, and after-tax, non-qualified investment accounts.

Asset location is important to help make use of tax efficiency in an investment portfolio. For example, stocks held in after-tax, non-qualified accounts for longer than one year as well as qualified dividends are taxed at more favorable LTCG rates. These rates range from 0%, 15%, and 20%. Taxable bond interest, however, is taxed as ordinary income, leaving an investor being taxed at potentially higher amounts – up to 37% in 2023.

As you know, amounts contributed to qualified, pre-tax accounts such as traditional IRAs, 401(k)s, etc., are taxed as ordinary income when withdrawn from the respective plans. Even non-deductible IRAs have their earnings taxed as ordinary income when withdrawn.

Designated Roth accounts such as Roth IRAs and Roth 401(k)s are funded with after-tax contributions and qualified withdrawals are tax free. In other words, by contributing to Roth accounts, you're taxed on the contributions now, with earnings received tax free in retirement – when you may potentially be in a higher tax bracket.

In a perfect world, an investor would want to hold all their assets in Roth accounts. This way they could take advantage of tax-free distributions from the Roth accounts. Alas, it's not a perfect world! Some individuals may not qualify for Roth IRAs (their income is too high) or they may only have access to a Roth 401(k) where their contributions are limited ($19,000 to $25,000 depending on age).

Once you've reached the contribution limits in your 401(k) or IRA, you'll likely want to make additional investments in stocks, stock mutual funds, and ETFs for tax efficiency.

It makes sense to hold bonds (including bond mutual funds and ETFs) in tax-qualified accounts and Roth accounts. One caveat, however, is municipal bonds. Generally, these should not be held in tax-qualified accounts as their interest is already exempt from federal taxation, and potentially state and local taxation.

After-Tax Investment Considerations

Some individuals can contribute after-tax amounts to their employer-sponsored plans such as a tax-deferred 401(k) or a defined benefit pension. Since these amounts are after-tax, the contributions start adding up to a sizeable amount known as basis. Basis is simply the amount of after-tax money put into these accounts that is not taxed when it's withdrawn. Earnings on the basis are taxable.

Individuals considering contributing after-tax amounts to the above plans may also consider if it makes sense to contribute to a non-qualified account. Like the aforementioned employer-sponsored plans, contributions to a non-qualified account are made with after-tax dollars, building a sizable basis, which is not taxed when withdrawn. Also, like the above employer-sponsored accounts, any earnings are subject to taxation. The major difference is in the way the earnings from the non-qualified account are taxed.

Earnings on after-tax contributions to employer-sponsored plans are taxed at the individual's ordinary income tax rate. However, earnings on after-tax contributions to a non-qualified account are taxed more favorably as LTCG (assuming they are held for longer than one year). Although the non-qualified account may seem like the way to go, there are several items to consider before choosing which account to place your after-tax money.

One area to explore is how retirement income is taxed in your state. Some states such as Illinois currently do not tax retirement income. Thus, the earnings from the after-tax 401(k) or pension contributions would not be taxed at the state level, only federally. Earnings from the non-qualified account would be taxed both at the state and federal level.

Additionally, consider who bears the risk in the different plans. Most non-qualified account and employer-sponsored 401(k) risk is the responsibility of the individual or employee. Some defined benefit pension plans bear all the investment risk. Thus, if an employer-sponsored defined benefit pension allows after-tax contributions, credits interest at 7.5% (accurate as of this writing for some pensions), and bears all the investment risk, an individual may find that they are willing to pay a higher percentage in tax for the corresponding interest rate credit and transfer of investment risk.

Other considerations include your goals for the money at retirement and at death. For example, a 401(k) will have RMDs at age 70 ½. Non-qualified accounts will not. Furthermore, most beneficiaries that inherit a 401(k) account must take RMDs based on the life expectancy of the beneficiary. Taxation is still at the ordinary income tax rate on earnings, but the after-tax amounts still constitute basis.

Beneficiaries of non-qualified accounts experience a change in their tax basis. In other words, the account value on the date of the account owner's death becomes the beneficiary's new tax basis. Thus, any earnings above that amount are taxed at LTCG rates.

For defined benefit pensions, the beneficiary would be the spouse. At the death of the account owner, the spousal beneficiary would receive whatever annuity payout was agreed upon when the pension started. However, if the employee was single or the spousal beneficiary dies; these payments generally cease. There's no account balance to inherit nor additional beneficiary to receive the pension.

Amending Your Tax Return

Not much needs to be done after you've filed your taxes except for deciding to have more withheld in the future if you had to write a check to Uncle Sam or deciding what to do with the refund (hint: pay yourself first) if you received a refund.

What happens when your return may have been submitted with mistakes or perhaps costly errors? If the error is minor the IRS will correct errors or accept returns without certain forms or schedules attached.

For returns that have a change in filing status, income, deductions, credits, or major errors, then filing an amended return will most likely be appropriate. To file an amended return, you can file using form 1040X. Form 1040X will allow corrections to earlier filed returns that used 1040A or 1040EZ.

If you to file for separate years, then a separate 1040X must be filed for each tax year that's being amended.
According to the IRS keep the following points in mind:

- *Attach copies of any forms or schedules that are being changed because of the amendment, including any Form(s) W-2 received after the original return was filed.*
- *Tax forms can be obtained by calling 800-829-3676 or visiting www.irs.gov.*
- *An amended tax return cannot be filed electronically under the e-file system.*
- *Normal processing time for Forms 1040X is up to 12 weeks from the IRS receipt date.*

If claiming a refund, the amended return needs to be filed within 3 years after the due date of your original return or 3 years after the date you filed your return if you filed for an extension.

What To Do If You're a Victim of Tax Fraud

Hopefully this will never happen to you but in the unfortunate event you become of victim of tax fraud there are some steps that you can take to help alleviate the concern that someone has stolen your identity to file a fraudulent tax return to receive the refund.

Generally, the first sign of fraud appears when you try to file your return electronically. Most e-file providers receive acknowledgements from the IRS that the return was successfully e-filed. If a return is rejected, a code will return with the rejection indicating what the issue is.

For example, a sign of fraud will indicate that the Social Security numbers used to file your return were previously used in the same tax year for another return. If you know you didn't previously file, then fraud is likely.

If you feel you're the victim of fraud, here's what you can do:

- Contact the IRS immediately and let them know you feel you're the victim of fraud.

- Generally, you won't be able to e-file so instead you'll paper file your return. You or your tax preparer can provide a statement as to why you're paper filing and that you feel you've been a victim of fraud.

- Review all of your outside accounts and information to see if you can detect where the culprit got your information. Consider changing passwords and or limiting access to what information you provide.

Lastly, this is directly from the IRS:

The IRS has security measures in place to verify the accuracy of tax returns and the validity of Social Security numbers submitted.

- *If you receive a notice from the IRS that leads you to believe someone may have used your Social Security number fraudulently, please notify the IRS immediately by responding to the name and number printed on the notice or letter.*

- *If you are an actual or potential victim of identity theft and would like the IRS to mark your account to identify any questionable activity, please complete Form 14039, Identify Theft Affidavit. Mail or fax the form to the address or fax number listed on the notice with your tax return if your electronic filing was rejected or to the address/fax located in the instructions.*

- *You may also contact the IRS's Identity Protection Specialized Unit (IPSU) at 800-908-4490. IPSU employees are available to answer questions about identity theft and resolve any tax account issues that resulted from identity theft.*

- *Review Publication 4535, Identity Theft Prevention and Victim Assistance, for more information. It is available in both English and Spanish.*

- *If you suspect someone else is using your Social Security number, or to secure information on how to prevent identity theft, you can contact the Federal Trade Commission (FTC) Identity Theft Hotline toll-free at 877-438-4338.*

Hopefully this never happens to you, but if it does, there's a way to fix it.

Chapter 7 – Estate Planning

Estate Planning Essentials

Do you have an estate? If you think you have an estate, then please keep reading – this should be you and everyone else reading this. In other words, everyone has an estate.

Many individuals believe that to have an estate they must have a certain amount of "stuff", net worth, income, social status, etc. Furthermore, these same individuals may feel estate planning involves complex documents, high legal fees, and considerable time. While this may be true for some estate plans, it's not always the case.

Additionally, many individuals feel that estate planning involves planning for incapacity or death. Although not pleasant to discuss, planning for one's incapacity or death is an important part of their overall financial plan.

Having these discussions before incapacity arises (a possibility) or death occurs (a certainty) can help ease the stress for loved ones dealing with these situations if and when they happen. It may also help prevent arguing and discord among relatives who may act based on what they think you wanted versus what you actually want.

Besides planning for incapacity or death, estate planning can also involve the distribution of assets when people are alive and well. Many individuals need estate planning regarding gifting, philanthropy, taxation, etc.

Almost everyone needs some type of estate plan. The simplicity or complexity will depend on the vicissitudes pertaining to your individual or family situation.

The following is a list of some estate planning essentials that you may consider for your overall financial plan. Of course, it's highly recommended you seek the advice and assistance of a competent financial professional and or an attorney to help draft documents and align your estate plan to your overall financial plan.

- A will. A will is a legal document that allows you to choose which individuals get your possessions when you die. For parents, wills are imperative as they will determine who will become guardian of children if the parents pass away while the children are minors.

Dying without a will (called dying intestate) can be problematic. Without a will, the state of the deceased individual will determine distribution of assets, guardianship for minor children, etc. It can be a mess. A will can ensure that your wishes are carried out.

For parents: consider having discussions with those individuals you feel you'd want as guardians for your children. Make sure they agree and want to undertake this huge responsibility.

- A trust. A trust is another legal document that ensures that some type of property (called corpus) is administered in a certain way (generally your intentions) according to the verbiage in the trust.

  Some of the more common types of trusts involve trusts for minor children. If parents pass away, they may leave money to children to ensure financial stability for their upbringing. However, minor children are likely not going to be able to handle financial matters. A trust will have the money set aside for the children (the beneficiaries) but managed by an individual (the trustee) whom the parents deemed financially fit to distribute and use trust assets for the children.

Other types of trusts may be necessary depending on the situation. These involve special needs trusts for parents of special needs children, spendthrift trusts (to limit or prevent wasteful spending by beneficiaries), and charitable trusts (to carry out charitable intentions).

Lastly, trusts avoid the publicity of probate — which means that when your will is going through court, it becomes public knowledge. Trusts help keep information about those assets in the trust private.

- Powers of Attorney. Powers of attorney are documents designed to allow an individual to act on your behalf – generally in the event you cannot act on our own behalf. The two most common powers of attorney are powers of attorney for property and powers of attorney for health care.

  A power of attorney for property allows an individual to make financial decisions for you. This may include paying bills, financial transactions, etc. This power may be granted right away (when you're fully capable of making said decisions) or may be "springing" which means the power is granted when you become incapacitated.

A power of attorney for health care allows an individual to act on your behalf regarding medical decisions. In the event of your incapacitation, this document allows an individual you've chosen to make decisions for you regarding treatment, procedures, and, should the situation be that dire, whether to remain on life support.

If you're feeling uncomfortable reading this, imagine the discomfort a family faces with these decisions *without* these documents in place.

- Other advanced medical directives. Additional documents to consider include living wills, do not resuscitate orders (DNRs), and organ donation. Living wills provide a guide to the doctors or your power of attorney for health care regarding how you'd want to be treated medically and whether you would want to remain on life support.

Do not resuscitate orders tell medical professionals to not take life-saving measures – depending on the medical condition and per your wishes.

- Beneficiary designations. One of the easiest ways to estate plan is via your beneficiary designations on your life insurance policies, retirement plans (401k, IRAs, etc.), annuities, and investment accounts.

  Naming beneficiaries allows you to determine who receives those assets in the event of your death. Like trusts, beneficiary designations avoid the publicity of probate.

  A beneficiary designation can also work congruently with trusts. In other words, an individual can name a trust as their beneficiary on their life insurance (say, if they have minor children) and the trust then receives the life insurance proceeds and the trustee distributes the proceeds to the beneficiaries per the language in the trust.

If you're considering an estate plan or believe that your current plan needs updating (e.g. after a life event such as marriage, divorce, a birth, a death, etc.), talk to a financial professional and or your attorney. There are several do-it-yourself websites available, but to quote Abraham Lincoln, "He who represents himself has a fool for a client."

How Property Transfers at Death

When you die, the way in which your property is handled will depend on the type of documents (or lack thereof) you've set up before your death. The following is a summary of the ways your property transfers to heirs when you pass away.

Life Insurance. At death, life insurance proceeds are passed to your beneficiaries (and in most cases, tax free). For example, if you have a life insurance policy with a face amount of $500,000, when you die, your beneficiaries receive the $500,000 face amount tax free.

When you purchase life insurance, you name your beneficiary or beneficiaries – those who receive the death benefit when you die. Most married couples will name each other as beneficiaries on their respective polices, some will name charities, and other will name other relatives, individuals, or trusts.

Life insurance contracts generally avoid probate (the legal process of validating a will and division of property), unless you name your estate beneficiary (a bad idea) or fail to name a beneficiary (also a bad idea).

Annuities. At death annuities operate the same way as life insurance regarding beneficiaries. A big difference however, is the tax treatment. Even though an annuity may pay a death benefit, in most cases it is taxable to the beneficiary. This is different from life insurance death benefits that are received tax free. Any taxable annuity death benefits are taxed as ordinary income.

Trusts. Trusts can be established either during your lifetime or at your death. They may also be revocable (changeable) or irrevocable (not changeable). Trusts are set up by a grantor (the person wanting the trust) and assets are placed in the trust, managed by a trustee, for the benefit of the trust beneficiary. When you die, the assets in the trust are still managed by the trustee for the benefit of the beneficiary. Like annuities and life insurance, trusts avoid probate.

Brokerage Accounts. When you have a brokerage account where you hold stocks, bonds, mutual funds, or ETFs it's called a non-qualified brokerage account. The non-qualified means that it's not a 401(k) or IRA. When you open this type of account, you are given the option to name a beneficiary on the account should you die. At death, the property passes to the beneficiary. The beneficiary also receives special tax treatment on the account (covered in the next section). Brokerage accounts also avoid probate.

Retirement plans. When you have retirement plans such as 401(k)s and IRAs you also name beneficiaries who get the account assets when you die. The tax treatment of the assets will depend on the account (Roth or not), and what the beneficiary chooses to do with the assets (sell them all or take minimum distributions). Brokerage accounts avoid probate.

Wills. A will is a written legal document that directs how and to whom your assets are dispersed after your death. Wills also name a guardian(s) for minor children should both parents die. Wills also name an executor for your estate that helps direct where assets go, what assets to sell, and filing the final tax return for the deceased and or the estate.

As mentioned before, probate is the process of validating a will. Thus, it's a public process, and often long and expensive. Additionally, the documents mentioned above supersede the language in a will. In other words, if your will states that your kids get your IRA assets at your death, but your IRA beneficiary is another person or entity, the IRA overrides the language in the will.

Dying without a will means dying intestate. Dying intestate means that the state determines how your assets are divided, who gets them, and if you have minor children, who becomes their guardian.

Different states have different laws, but be assured, the laws may differ from what your intentions are or who you think should get your assets or be guardians. Don't risk it. If you don't have a will, or your beneficiaries named, consider taking care of this *today*.

An extremely important point not to be overlooked is the need to update your beneficiaries or documents whenever you have a life changing event. Life changes mean births, deaths, divorces, job changes, etc. For example, if you get divorced and remarry, and forget to change your beneficiary from your ex-spouse to your new spouse – and you die – your ex-spouse is still the beneficiary and gets the property. It is paramount to update your accounts, estate documents, insurance policies, and retirement plans to reflect any life changes.

To Gift or Inherit? Deciding When to Bequeath Assets

After beneficiaries are named and you understand how assets are distributed at death, we need to discuss the tax implications of gifted and inherited assets. The following is a description of the tax implications of non-qualified assets (those not in 401(k)s or IRAs) received by beneficiaries if gifted during lifetime or inherited after death.

Our example will use stocks in a brokerage account as the assets demonstrating the tax implications of assets gifted during lifetime or inherited at death.

Let's assume that an individual has a brokerage account and they initially purchased $250,000 worth of stock in the account. Several years have gone by and the account as grown to $500,000. For tax purposes the basis in the account is $250,000. The individual is contemplating gifting the account to their beneficiary.

If the individual decides to gift the account during their lifetime to their beneficiary, the beneficiary receives the assets and acquires the same tax basis as the original account owner. This transfer of basis, called carryover basis, means that if the beneficiary then sells any or all the stocks in the account, the beneficiary's tax basis is $250,000. So, if the beneficiary sold the entire account for its current value of $500,000, the taxable gain would be $250,000 – the difference between the carryover basis of $250,000 and the sales price of $500,000.

On the other hand, if the original account owner decides not to gift the account during their lifetime and instead waits until dying for the beneficiary to inherit the account, the beneficiary receives the assets and a new basis is established. This new basis, called a step-up (or step-to) in basis, means that the beneficiary's tax basis is the fair market value of the account assets on the account owner's date of death.

In this example, if the fair market value of the stocks is $500,000 when the account owner dies, the beneficiary's new tax basis is $500,000. Thus, if the beneficiary sold the account for $500,000, the tax liability to the beneficiary would be zero. Any gains or losses on the inherited $500,000 would be subject to short- or long-term gains and losses, depending on the beneficiary's holding period after inheriting the assets.

This same tax basis situation would apply to mutual funds, ETFs, real estate, and other non-qualified assets. Of course, the intentions of the individual gifting or leaving the assets after their death is entirely their prerogative – which may supersede regardless of the tax implications to the beneficiary.

Chapter 8 – Professional Advice

Why Hire a Professional?

You can do plenty of things yourself, but for many tasks like managing your hard-earned savings, you need the skill and expertise of a professional. Especially when it comes to your finances, the professional's fees are paltry compared to the value they bring.

For mundane tasks we know we can do ourselves, it's second nature to roll up our sleeves and get the job done. For more complicated endeavors, there is no way you can go it alone.

You need to hire an attorney to make a will or help with a divorce. A real estate agent can walk you through the buying or selling of a home. You can increase your wealth by working with a financial advisor on your investments, financial plan, or other money matters.

Some people say that some of these things can be done without the help of a pro. Granted there are plenty of do-it-yourself places for wills, trusts, investing, and medical care. But let the buyer beware.

People who prefer going solo usually argue that it saves money. Sometimes, they have trust issues, or they think they can do the job just as well if not better than the professional. Of course, a few DIY-ers get lucky, but many make unwise choices and don't realize the consequences until much later.

Take for example the person who does his or her own will online. Without an attorney or advisor to check it over, his or her heirs might belatedly find out that he made a mistake, or the will wasn't properly written, according to the state's laws.

In our business of financial planning, we see too many do-it-yourselfers play the stock market game by actively trading, watching cable news, and reading money magazines. Do these amateurs really think they have an edge over thousands of Wall Street analysts and institutional investors? No wonder so many of them lose money and make terrible bets.

What should we as consumers look for when we hire help with financial matters? Here are some basics to look for:

- **Education**. Are they qualified and educated in their field? What degrees or designations do they hold?

- **Tenure**. How long have they practiced?

- **Licensing**. Are there state or federal standards needed for them to work in their profession?

- **What don't they know?** Are they willing to admit when they aren't qualified to help? Look at it this way: A medical general practitioner doesn't give you brain surgery. You need a brain surgeon. Both are doctors, but both have very different professions and clients. Likewise, an accountant can't help you make financial plans or allocate your investments properly.

- **Code of ethics**. Do they adhere to one?

- **Transparency**. Do you understand what they do for you, how they do it and how they get paid?

This list is merely a good place to start. The main point is that you hire a professional for their expertise, experience, and professional judgment. You admit that you don't know everything, and you are ready to trust an expert to guide you.

In the long run, professionals save you money by avoiding mistakes, and saving you time and energy that you can spend on more important tasks.

How to Choose a Financial Planner/Wealth Manager/Advisor

Before you sign a contract or buy a product consider the following before choosing your financial planner.

- Make sure they're a CFP®. At the very minimum, a CERTIFIED FINANCIAL PLANNER™ has the met the education, exam, ethics, and experience requirements to be qualified to discuss your financial planning needs. Anyone can call themselves a financial planner, but not everyone is a CFP®. This should be the starting point of your search. Just because the planner is a CFP®, doesn't mean you should automatically work with them.

- Make sure they're a fiduciary. A fiduciary is legally required to act in your best interest – regardless of the financial outcome for the planner. Planners that have only a suitability requirement are not required to act in your best interest, but merely find a product suitable for your situation. In other words (and these are my words) they only need to *rationalize* why the product is a good fit for you, but it may not be in your best interest. Some planners are required to act in their company's interest first, which means your best interests are secondary.

- Make sure they're fee-only. This means that the planner's only source of compensation is directly from you and not from the commissions on the sale of mutual funds or insurance products. That is, you pay them directly for advice and they work for you. Fee-only can be an hourly rate, retainer, or a percent fee on your money if they invest your money for you.

- Make sure your personalities mesh. Nothing's worse than getting butterflies every time you must meet with your planner or your planner being reluctant to return your call. The relationship should be professional, yet enjoyable and even fun. Sometimes personalities don't click and sometimes they mesh perfectly. Life's too short and your money too hard-earned to be uneasy talking with your planner. The good news is that if the planner lines up with the first three points above, it becomes easier to focus on the relationship and building trust together.

Interview a few planners that meet the descriptions above and see which one you like best.

Advisors: Trust but Verify

You can never be too careful with the major matters of life – especially your financial future. Take a lesson in caution from a former U.S. president and the heavily armed guards at the gates of a military facility. Trust but verify your financial advisor's bona fides.

I have the honor to provide financial counseling to service members, going to military installations to talk to soldiers and their families regarding financial issues such as buying a home, saving for retirement, reducing debt, or creating a budget.

On my first assignment, in late 2012, I pulled up to the base entrance – a heavily fortified gate – and the military police asked me to park to the side while they ran my identification and searched my vehicle for contraband. (Having MPs, armed with automatic weapons, searching you is humbling yet cool.)

A few months ago, I pulled up to the gate and a soldier I now know and recognize greeted me. When I handed him my ID, he said, "I know who you are, sir, and welcome back." He then went on to say, "I'm sorry sir, but I'm going to have to ask you to pull your vehicle over, open the doors, hood, glove box, and console and please turn off your engine. I know you've been here many times, but we have to follow protocol."

President Ronald Reagan, regarding nuclear arms inspections with the Soviet Union, once said the U.S. pledged to "Trust, but verify." Through almost two years on this military base, I built rapport and trust. They still verify.

The same saying holds true for your financial planner, insurance agent, advisor or other money professional. Verify his or her facts, recommendations and reports. I'm not saying never trust your professional or be overly leery – but it's OK to check work, advice and numbers every so often.

I encourage clients to check me out independently. One of the first sites I recommend: the Financial Industry Regulatory Authority's BrokerCheck service, an excellent way to look at a financial advisor's history, record and possible affiliations with other companies. Check the backgrounds of fee-only advisors on the site of the U.S. Securities and Exchange Commission.

If he or she is a CFP®, or holds some other designation, verify the sheepskin. Check the CFP Board for that designation, for example.

Verifying numbers and returns can be trickier but is certainly doable. Investigate on your own and, if you feel comfortable, get a second opinion. Ask your advisor about gross versus net returns, fees, expenses, and an advisor's method of compensation.

Morningstar ranks as a great avenue to investigate mutual funds, stocks, bonds and portfolio allocations.

Finally, trust your gut. If something sounds too good to be true, it usually is. If something doesn't make sense to you, it probably doesn't make sense, period. And if the advisor, agent, or professional can't explain how a financial product works or other important details, run.

Verification trumps trust.

5 Questions to Ask Your Advisor

If you're contemplating hiring a financial planner or advisor or if you're currently working with one, here are some fair and important questions you may consider asking him or her.

- Are you a fiduciary? Being a fiduciary means that the adviser must legally act in your best interest. While not an absolute guarantee that the advisor will never act otherwise, most advisors who are fiduciaries embrace the responsibility – they want to be fiduciaries. Any other answer than yes to this question means you need to keep searching for an advisor who is.

- How are you paid? Generally, three different answers will follow. It will either be fee-only, fee and commission, or commission. If the advisor says fee-based or salary, you'll want to dig deeper. These two responses don't say how the compensation is derived. More importantly, you want to know how you will pay the advisor. And if you're curious, exactly how much. Fee-only means the advisor is compensated directly from you, the client via hourly, retainer, or asset under management fees. Fee and commission is a combination of asset or hourly fees and commissions from product sales. Commission is derived from the sale of products. If the advisor is unsure – move on.

- What value do you provide relative to the money you're paid? Like the question says, this is relative. Cheap to one person may be expensive to another. Regardless of how much is paid, make sure you're receiving value. If you're unsure, ask the adviser to write it down for you. Good advisors may well be worth the money you pay – and then some.

- What are your credentials? Ask your advisor what credentials and education they have obtained to be able to work with you and your situation professionally. Many advisors have designations, and some will also have degrees specific to financial planning. Degrees specific to financial planning include bachelor's and master's degrees in financial planning or services, consumer finance, wealth management, and family economics among others. Specific designations to financial planning include the CFP®. The CFP® is considered the gold standard in financial planning designations.

- What conflicts or potential conflicts of interest exist? If the advisor only gets paid if you're sold a product, that's a conflict. If they only get paid if you move assets to their firm, that's a conflict. Conflicts are everywhere. They should and need to be disclosed – preferably in writing. Ask your advisor how he or she will mitigate or avoid conflicts of interest. If the conflicts are incongruent with your beliefs and values, find an advisor that is a better fit. It's important to note that just because there's a conflict does not mean the advisor is wrong or unethical.

Hopefully these questions will help provide a baseline to start the conversation with your advisor. Surely more will arise in your conversations, and that's to be expected.

How Advisors Get Paid

When you first meet with a financial advisor, it's important to ask not only how much his or her fees are, but *who* actually pays. An advisor's compensation method can affect the type of advice you get, so you should understand the differences before you choose who to hire.

There are three basic ways financial advisors and planners are compensated: Commissions, fees, and a combination of both.

Here is what makes them different and relevant to you as a client.

Commission. Some advisors get paid based on the products they sell. Commission rates vary between 5% and 50%, depending on the product. Term life insurance, for example, usually gives the advisor a commission of roughly 40% of the annual premium for the first year. Whole life insurance is generally 50% the first year. Term life policies, which cover you for a limited number of years, cost far less than whole life policies, which continue if you pay the premiums and accumulates a cash value. But the commission on a whole life policy is far greater than term.

Other commissioned products include annuity products, individual stocks and bonds purchased through a broker, auto, home, umbrella insurance, and mutual funds. Some mutual funds that charge a load or commission on the initial purchase, or back-loaded funds that charge you upon redeeming the investment.

Fee & Commission. Fee and commission (sometimes called fee-based) is essentially a combination of commissions and fees. A fee and commission advisor gets paid on commissions on certain products, and receives a fee on planning, advice, or investment management.

For example, an advisor who sells life insurance and annuities and does investment management collects commissions for the life and annuity products and takes a flat fee or percentage of the assets in the investment management account. Some products are fee-based but pay the advisor a commission to sell them.

Say you sign up for an asset management account where the annual fee is 2% to have your money professionally invested. You may only see a 2% charge for your fee, but the advisor who sold you the program may receive a commission. He or she should be forthcoming about this – regardless of you asking. Examples like this are seen in proprietary asset management programs of various companies and brokers. In both circumstances, the advisor is compensated by the product sold.

Fee-only. Fee-only advisors are paid for their advice, not on products. Payment comes a few different ways. The first is strictly on an hourly basis or on retainer, like an attorney. They may give you an estimate with a range of costs before providing advice and services.

Another way that advisors get paid is a flat fee for any assets of yours that they manage and invest for you. This can be as little as 0.25% or as high as 2%, depending on how much you invest. Some planners require a minimum level of assets to work with them and some do not. Most have a graduated fee schedule where your fee decreases as you invest more.

Many fee-only advisors offer to take you "off the clock" meaning that once you are billed by assets under management, they no longer charge you by the hour for advice and questions. Be careful of advisors that charge fees for both managing your money and hourly for planning. Make sure the advice is worth the extra money.

Fee-only is very transparent, meaning that you see exactly what you're paying and what you paid for on your quarterly statement.

Lastly, always read the fine print and know exactly what you pay for. An advisor's compensation doesn't include the expense ratios and fees of the investments he puts you in. You might hire a fee-only advisor but if he or she uses a mutual fund that charges 1.5% in expenses, don't be surprised when you see more than the advisor's 1% fee siphoned off. A commissioned advisor could sell you an annuity that has fund fees of 1.5% and policy charges of another 1.25%. This is another 2.75% of charges annually in addition to the commissions the advisor collects.

Your best approach is to be up-front: Ask about commissions and fees before you agree to buy a financial product. Have the advisor tell you how much he or she gets paid for convincing you to do something. If you don't like what you hear or don't understand the answer, think about seeking another advisor's services. A good professional deserves to get paid, but his or her main goal should be to make more of your money work for you, not themselves. All three compensation types have their advantages and disadvantages. It all comes down to what sort of service you need and who you are comfortable with.

Do your homework, ask lots of questions.
Any advisor, no matter how they get paid, should
put your interests first and only make
recommendations that are best for your personal
situation.

Do Unto Others?

In the financial services industry there has been considerable discussion on the application of the fiduciary standard of care for clients versus the suitability standard of care. There are generally two sides to the argument: on the fiduciary side the standard of care is to act in the best interests of the client and the other side which is a suitability standard of care in which the recommendation needs to be suitable, but not necessarily in the best interest of the client.

This is where things get sticky.

Acting in your best interest is pretty cut and dry. After extensive questioning and gathering of information a recommendation is made to you based on what is best for your situation. This means recommending keeping your current course of action, following a designed and carefully thought out plan, or recommending you do business elsewhere.

Suitability requires only finding an appropriate solution that suits you. This may be a proprietary product that the advisor is only able to sell based on company and contract affiliation, licensing, and compensation structure. In other words (and these are my words only) the advisor may *rationalize* the reason for the recommendation regardless if it's in your best interest.

Proponents of the suitability standard are normally compensated by commissions only or a combination of commission and fees. They are normally adamant about only adhering to the suitability standard. Why? The answer is simple: self-preservation.

Think of it this way, if the only way you're compensated is through the sales of a product then why would you want to be held to a standard that says what you're selling must be in the best interest of the client? What if you can only sell life insurance or annuities? As the saying goes, if you all you have is a hammer then everything looks like a nail.

Proponents of the fiduciary standard are dominantly compensated by fees directly from you. What does this mean? This means you pay the advisor for their advice, not a product sale. The relationship nor the compensation of the advisor isn't tied to a sale it's tied to the quality of advice. In other words, it's very transparent. You know exactly what you're paying for and can rest assured you're getting advice regardless of a product sale. In this case the advisor has a tool box full of tools to utilize instead of just one tool.

Admittedly this type of system is not 100% perfect. There will still be a few bad apples and there will always be outliers, and there will be bad advice. However, from personal experience I have been able to witness both sides. Early in my financial career I worked for a firm that was commission only – one of those firms where I was told if the client wasn't going to buy, send them to the 800 number.

Really.

Temptation to sell something, anything to make a living was high. I was arguably the worst salesperson they had. It's extremely difficult to be a fiduciary in that situation – not impossible, but difficult.

Being able to work with a firm that is aligned with my own beliefs and embracing the fiduciary standard there is little, if any temptation to recommend anything less than what's best for the client. No sales pressure, no product pushing.

For those that would argue against the fiduciary standard let me ask this question. It's a question I ask frequently of students and colleagues that argue in favor of a suitability standard.

"If roles were reversed and you were the client, what standard would you want applied to you?"

They answer almost always the fiduciary standard.

The next question is rhetorical, but apt:

"They why should your clients get anything less than what you want for yourself?"

There's usually silence.

Advice to the Masses May Not Apply to You

Occasionally, I will tune in to a nationally syndicated talk show regarding personal finance. The host is very popular among listeners and has written several best sellers. Many individuals follow the financial program designed to educate individuals on how to set a budget, get out of debt, and save for retirement. The advice given is applicable to many individuals. Many times, it's excellent advice.

Sometimes it's not.

A listener called into the show and explained that she had approximately $100,000 in an annuity, in an IRA. The annuity paid an interest rate of 2% and had a current surrender charge of 4% - just over $4,000. The caller was asking the host whether she should surrender the annuity and roll it over to a non-annuity IRA invested in mutual funds.

In a matter of seconds, the recommendation was to surrender the annuity, pay the surrender charges of over $4,000, and find a mutual fund that pays 6%. The reasoning was that if the annuity was paying 2% and the surrender charge was 4%, the caller would need to find a fund that makes 6% to "break even."

There are a few things not necessarily ideal in this situation. First, why wouldn't the advice be to wait out the surrender period and still receive 2% interest? This was a guaranteed 2% rate! Not a lot but guaranteed. Second, why pay 4% in surrender charges to move from a guaranteed rate to a vehicle (mutual fund) that is not guaranteed? Admittedly, if the caller was looking for a higher potential rate of return, moving to a riskier investment may make sense. However, the host could have advised the caller to wait until the surrender period was over to make the move.

Finally, the caller doesn't realize that moving their money to one of the host's endorsed providers ensures they'll get a commissioned salesperson offering them front-loaded (commission) mutual funds. Many commissioned funds have a common break point (the point at which front end loads are reduced) for $100,000 in assets which is 3.5%. This means that when the investor moves out of her annuity, she's losing the 2% guarantee, 4% in surrender charges, and another 3.5% in front end loads (commissions).

In other words, the investor would need to find a fund that would make her 9.5% in the first year *just to break even*. The advice on finding a mutual fund that pays 6% was not only inaccurate (mutual funds

don't have guaranteed rates) but the advice on only
needing 6% to break even was erroneous!

I do agree that the annuity should be rolled over to a
non-annuity IRA. An IRA annuity is overkill. You
have a tax-deferred vehicle (the IRA) in a tax-
deferred wrapper (the annuity). However, perhaps
the advice would have been better if the host would
have told the client to wait until the surrender
charges were done (about a year or two) and then
roll it over. On the host's recommendation she'll be
out approximately $9,400 (9.5% based off 6% lost in
total from surrendering the annuity, and another
3.5% on the approximately $96,000 moved to the
endorsed provider) and will need to make that in one
year just to get into the black.

The advice in many TV, radio shows, and
publications may be good for individuals needing to
get out from under credit card debt or get control of
their personal finances. There are some universal
truths in personal finance. However, this situation
identifies an area of concern for those who
otherwise wouldn't know the true cost of the advice
they're receiving.

Additionally, most, if not all these talk show hosts,
journalists, etc. are not fiduciaries – they don't have
to put your best interests first. They are not held to

the same legal standard of a fiduciary. Most of them aren't licensed to provide financial planning advice, products, and services.

Your individual wealth management plan will require more than a one-size-fits-all-solution.

Advisors Aren't Clairvoyant

My firm's clients and prospective clients often ask us which direction the market is going. This is always an entertaining question – and some of our longtime clients already know the answer. While advisors can't predict the future, they can help you prepare for it to make the best out of what the markets throw at you.

I have a bit of a sense of humor, so I often joke that the day they handed out crystal balls in my investment class, it was the one time I called in sick. You only get one chance at the coveted crystal ball. Thus, I forever lost the opportunity to predict the future of the markets. Darn.

Whether you find that joke funny or not, the takeaway is that nobody can predict the future, especially in securities markets. No matter how experienced and savvy advisors are, we can never make good predictions or time the markets, and you should be wary of those who claim they can. But this doesn't mean we can't plan ahead.

So why do we invest? Why do we save for retirement? Why do we prepare for the future? The reason is because we can certainly have a great idea of where we are going and where we want to be. We understand that over the long run, it's likely that our nest egg and the contributions to it over the years grows, so that when it comes time to retire and actually live the future that we planned for, it's livable and enjoyable. This is why we plan ahead and seek out financial advisors for help.

Of course, there are always the naysayers that worry that the market might crash, taking all of their money away. I always answer, "What if it does? So what?" A good planner never puts immediate or near-term money at substantial risk, so that isn't likely. We don't need a crystal ball to reasonably assess risk in a client's portfolio.

Good planners take the time to discuss your strategy and goals. Based on your appetite for risk, they properly allocate your investment assets so that fluctuations don't wipe out your savings.

We can tell you that the market always eventually tanks and recovers. And that's why, based on an individual's plan, we allocate and manage accordingly. So, technically we can predict the future, but we just can't tell you the exact dates crashes and recoveries happen, and we don't pretend that we can.

Letting market fluctuations scare you away from saving and investing is like avoiding the doctor for fear of hearing about a serious medical condition. Your doctor tells you to eat right, exercise and refrain from tobacco or excessive drinking to live longer. You might follow the doctor's advice and still get a cold or you may get seriously injured in an accident. By the same token, a good financial plan doesn't inoculate your savings against market dips and crashes. But you and the market eventually recover. We can't predict how long recovery takes, but we can make investments prudently.

Overall, we take our doctor's advice because we plan to live a long and happy life, even if we get hurt now and again. The same is true with professional financial advice. Anything can happen, but we plan for the future as best we can.

Chapter 9 – Potpourri

Like the title says, this chapter is a mix of different material that didn't quite fit into the previous chapters but is still relevant and hopefully beneficial for you.

Advice I Would Give My Younger Self

A lot has changed over the last 40 years. Smartphones are part of our regular vocabulary, millions of individuals do their shopping online, and markets are still unpredictable.

Naturally, I've changed over the last 40 years. If I had a DeLorean that could take me back in time, I'd try to impart some wisdom on my younger self.

Unfortunately, the closest thing I have to a DeLorean is a silver mini-van (with sliding rather than gull wing doors) lacking a flux capacitor. My hope is that younger readers can benefit from what I am about to tell my younger self.

- From the moment you start earning money, save at least 15% of what you make. Whether it's mowing lawns or stocking shelves you have the gift of time to your advantage; and you never get it back.

- Don't be afraid to live frugally. It's not how you spend that will impress people, it's your character.

- When you go on dates, it's OK to pick up the tab; but it's also OK if you go Dutch. It's also OK to if you don't spend any money on a date. Sometimes a simple stroll through a park along a river will do more for a relationship than dinner and a movie.

- Give to others who need it and do it without fanfare (e.g. virtue signaling). Random acts of kindness and generosity compound more powerfully than you could ever imagine.

- One of the smartest financial decisions you made was waiting to go to college. You didn't know it at the time, but you weren't ready. A few years of maturity will prepare you to be a better student, and you'll appreciate college and your instructors more.

- Drive your 1985 Pontiac Sunbird until it completely dies. You'll save so much by not having a car payment. See the second bullet point.

- Hold off on applying for a credit card. There's plenty of time and you don't need one now.

- I know it hurts to hear this, but your parents were right. You may know everything now, but as you age, you'll get dumber. That's a good thing.

- Money doesn't buy happiness. You need some to live comfortably, but after a certain point, your happiness with having more money increases at a decreasing rate. If this is confusing, sit in the front of the class when you take Economics 101 in college.

- You will have regrets. Don't dwell on them. Learn from them.

- You will learn a lot by failing. Get ready for some whoppers.

- Try your best to think before you speak or act. This will benefit you more than you know.

- Success is not defined by what you have or what you do. It's defined by who you are.

- Count your blessings. Two of them call you dad. Be grateful for everything you have.

Income ≠ Wealth

There's a big difference between income and wealth. Income can be considered the amount of money you earn on a consistent basis. For most individuals, this is a paycheck. Wealth can be considered your net worth, or, more specifically, how much income your wealth generates and how long you can sustain a given lifestyle without having to receive a conventional paycheck.

Some individuals may confuse the two. Some may feel that a high income equates to wealth. They may also think that to be wealthy or to generate wealth, their income must be high. This isn't the case. While a high income may help to build wealth faster, it is no guarantee that an individual is or will be wealthy.

Let's look at an example of two couples, about the same age, nearing retirement and wondering if they have enough wealth to do so. These are based on two of my actual client interactions, although some info will be generalized to maintain anonymity.

The first couple, Hank and Bess, has saved roughly $3 million in retirement accounts. They are both in their mid-50s and neither earned more than $50,000 annually throughout their careers. This couple is debt-free, while owning two vehicles, two homes, a business (purchased with cash just before retirement) and needs about $38,000 annually to meet their retirement expenses – half of which will be covered by their Social Security when they take it.

Conservatively, this couple needs to earn just over half of a percent (.00633) annually to cover the $19,000 needed for their expenses, from their $3 million portfolio, while leaving the principal untouched. This couple is *very* wealthy.

The second couple, Stan and Kat, currently still work and earn about $750,000 annually. They have a big house with a mortgage, no kids, and make payments on two luxury sedans. They make quite a bit of money annually and their lifestyle shows it.

However, when considering retirement, this couple's wealth – what they have currently saved to support their wanted retirement lifestyle, would last them about 13 years.

On the outside, it may look like Stan and Kat are very wealthy. However, compared to Hank and Bess, their wealth is quite low. Unless they change their lifestyle, or saving habits, Stan and Kat's retirement outlook is grim.

Income does not equate to wealth. As you can see from the examples above, it doesn't take a huge income to build wealth. It takes discipline to save, avoid unnecessary debt, and delay gratification to become wealthy.

Frugality Versus Frugal Spending

Let's discuss the difference between being frugal and frugal spending. I think it really boils down to the mindset of the individual. Frugality, in my opinion, is making smart purchases when necessary, and forgoing purchasing altogether if not. I also believe that frugality is making purchases that reduce the need to spend more in the future (i.e. buying a quality product for more money in order to reduce or eliminate repair expenses in the future).

Frugal spending, on the other hand, is buying something simply because it's on sale or cheap – regardless of need. For example, many times we see items in the store advertised as "buy one, get one half off" or "Two for $5". It can be easy to fall into this trap of buying these items and leaving the store feeling good about having saved money. Sometimes we may even think that because we bought two items and one was half priced, that we saved money. This only makes sense if we needed the two items to begin with.

Let's look at the "buy one, get one half off" deal. This may make sense frugally if you truly need two of the items. Otherwise, if you only need one, purchasing the other for half price is still wasting money. The other argument is buying something simply because it was on sale. Again, if the item isn't needed, then you're saving zero money, and in fact, wasting money buying the item even if it's on sale.

In other words, if an item is normally priced $30, and you buy it on sale for $20 but don't need it, you've still wasted $20. You haven't "saved" $10. The fact that it was on sale is irrelevant. It simply makes you feel better for spending less. In this example, it's only $10.

But, ten bucks is ten bucks.

As items get more expensive, this concept only grows larger. Bigger purchases just mean you're wasting more money, not saving more. This applies to housing, cars, and even buying in bulk at the warehouse store.

The good news is that we can start on the smaller items and build our self-discipline from there. By practicing frugality, we can learn to resist the urge to spend, even if it's on sale.

How to Really Buy a Car

Buying a car (notice I didn't say *new* car) is an event many individuals experience throughout their lifetime. Personally, I have had several cars in my lifetime, and I'm sure I'll have a few more (right now the ol' mini-van stands at 331,000 miles). My goal is not to spend too much on a depreciating asset, yet make a sensible purchase based on reliability, fuel efficiency, and insurance costs. Although some readers may not agree with me, here are some tips on how to really buy a car.

- Do your homework. Websites such as Kelly Blue Book (kbb.com), Consumer Reports, and Edmunds.com have valuable information on used car prices, reliability reports, known recalls, expert and buyer reviews, and what to expect at the dealership. In addition, obtaining information from these websites gives you bargaining power when you go to purchase your vehicle at a dealership or from a private party.

- Never, ever walk into a dealership and tell them your monthly payment you're hoping to get. In fact, don't tell them if they ask you.

Instead, negotiate the price of the car first. Many dealerships are more than happy to get you the payment you want, while not helping you consider total cost, interest on financing, etc.

- Try to never, ever have a car payment. Think of it this way: you're making monthly interest and principal payments on a depreciating asset. If you can, hold off on the purchase until you've saved enough cash to buy the car outright. This also gives you more negotiating power knowing you can walk away from the deal and buy the same car at a different dealership. And no, you don't need a new car every five years.

- Don't buy the hype. Just about every dealership offers the same discounts and pricing. The reason is that other than freight charges, most dealerships pay the *same* for the new vehicles going on their lots.

- If you can, avoid buying a new car. Consider this; an individual making $100,000 in annual income who purchases a $30,000 new car just spent 30% (nearly a third) of their income on a depreciating asset. There are plenty of reliable, used cars that are in perfect working condition. In fact, take advantage of the fact that the used car has already had much of its depreciation absorbed by the previous owner.

Furthermore, I have seen too many individuals buy a new car, finance it, then end up upside down on the car. This means they owe more than the car is worth. To make matter worse, some individuals wreck their cars, have nothing to drive, yet still must make payments. Ick.

- Buy your car before you *have* to. I'm not suggesting you buy a car you don't need. What I am suggesting is that you have the car you want ready to purchase when you need to. That is, if your current vehicle breaks down or is no longer running, you know you can get the vehicle you researched, instead of making a fast, emotional decision that will likely cost you more money.

- Avoid leasing. This never made sense to me. Often the rationale is "if you want new car every three years, then leasing is the way to go." Baloney. Leasing is simply making a car payment on an asset you *don't* own. Save up and buy the car outright. As mentioned earlier, you don't need a new car every five years, and you certainly don't need one every three.

- The exhilaration of the purchase wears off fast. Buy a car that's affordable, practical, reliable, and fuel efficient. Forget about what the Joneses have or what they think. Take what you would have paid for the monthly payment and put it toward retirement, college, or saving for a house.

- Insurance matters. Especially if you're young, insurance on vehicles matters. The price of insurance on a used sports car is much more expensive than a used sedan. In addition, lenders will often require that you have insurance to protect their asset (it is theirs since you borrowed their money to buy it) including comprehensive and collision which adds to premium amounts. Generally, the older, less sporty the car, the lower insurance premiums.

- Avoid the extended warranties. In most cases, these warranties are not needed. Instead, use the aforementioned sites to research the vehicle's reliability so you don't need to purchase the warranty. Finally, should a major repair be necessary, simply use your emergency fund or rainy-day fund to pay for the repairs. Also, a major repair doesn't indicate you need a new vehicle. Quantify the cost of the repair versus a purchasing a different vehicle. Often, the price of the repair will outweigh purchasing a different vehicle altogether. Sometimes, repairs can be made by you. With a little elbow grease and YouTube, you'd be surprised at what you can do, and how much you can save.

Buy Assets

How you choose to spend or invest your money can have an impact on your net worth. Many of you are familiar with the net worth equation which is Assets – Liabilities = Net Worth. In other words, what you own, minus what you owe, equals what's yours.

However, what is conventional wisdom isn't always what's best. What I mean is, just because something is generally known as an "asset" doesn't mean it's going to help your wealth. Here are a few examples.

- Your house. While generally considered an asset, and to some, an investment, your home can also drain you of net worth and cash flow. Homes need upkeep, repairs, insurance, utilities, taxes, and many have mortgage payments. Additionally, your home does not produce any free cash flow. There's also no guarantee your home will appreciate (it may even depreciate). However, paying down your mortgage will generally help your net worth.

- Your car. Let me be blunt. Your car is a wasting asset. It depreciates over time and in many cases, ends up costing you more that you paid for it. Vehicle loans aside, cars need insurance, gas, maintenance, and upkeep. A loan on a vehicle is making payments on a depreciating asset. Like your home, your vehicle produces zero cash flow.

- Your things. Your things include furniture, knick-knacks, toys, appliances, etc. Like vehicles, they generally depreciate. Like your home and vehicles, they produce zero cash flow.

The reason I mention the above examples is to encourage you to think of buying true assets, if your goal is to increase your wealth. True assets appreciate and may provide cash flow. Here are some examples.

- Stocks and bonds. Stocks represent ownership of a company and provide cash flow via dividends. Bonds represent owning a company's debt and provide cash flow in the form of interest payments. Additionally, you can own multiple stocks and bonds with mutual funds or ETFs – which pass the cash flows and appreciation to their investors.

- Real estate. By real estate, I do not mean your home. I mean real estate that produces cash flow such as commercial properties or residential rental real estate. Real estate also provides tax advantages through depreciation, like-kind exchanges, and other business expenses.

- A business. Owning a business may provide opportunities to create cash flow and potential tax advantages through business deductions. Additionally, businesses that provide value (in addition to cash flow) can also be sold for profit.

- Education. Education via college, internships, or self-education can increase your knowledge, human capital, and can increase your cash flow through promotions, pay increases, and intellectual capital.

By focusing on true assets – those that can provide cash flow and potential for appreciation can have a beneficial impact on your net worth and wealth. While it's not a bad thing to have a home, furniture, vehicles, etc. (I own these), if your goal is to increase your wealth and net worth, consider focusing on true assets.

Multiple Income Streams

This information can be used if you're looking to boost income to increase retirement savings, pay off debt earlier, or simply to put yourself in a better position financially.

In financial planning we often talk about risk management as one of the bricks to the foundation of any solid financial plan. As you've read earlier, risk management consists of auto, home, life, disability, and other insurance coverage in addition to an emergency fund.

Another area of "insurance" would be creating additional or multiple income streams as a hedge against losing an income source due to downsizing, termination, etc. If none of these negative events occurs, then the extra income can be used to bolster retirement savings, reduce debt, or save extra for college. The point is that if one job dissolves there are other income streams providing cash flow.

The question then becomes how to find these additional income streams or "pipelines". One of the easiest would be to simply find another part-time job, preferably doing something you enjoy. This could be working at your child's school as an aid, waiting tables an earning extra money in tips, or simply working hourly on the evenings or weekends at a local business.

Other income streams include dividends and interest from your investments, income from real estate and rental properties, and royalties from publications or patents.

You may also consider starting you own business, part-time, to generate additional income. One area to look is as an offshoot to what you're currently doing. For example, if you're a teacher, you may also find it enjoyable to do consulting to teachers and schools in an area of expertise. As an accountant, you could find extra work from January through April doing tax returns.

The main idea here is to leverage your current knowledge and expertise into another income stream. The learning curve is less onerous. From a tax perspective, the IRS allows certain deductions if you have a legitimate business and business expenses.

One area of caution: be careful of starting a business that relies on you working hard to make someone else money (i.e. multi-level or network marketing organizations). Often these types of "businesses" recruit naïve individuals to sell their products and recruit others to the "pyramid". Generally, those making any substantial income are those at the top of the pyramid (i.e. the founders).

Financial Counseling Before and After Marriage

Many individuals who are dating and growing closer together learn more and more about the other person. Habits (good and bad) likes, dislikes, and traits all make themselves known at some point in the relationship.

Before getting married, many individuals choose to seek counseling. This can help answer questions about whether they are doing the right thing, religious reasons, etc. Some couples choose to continue this counseling into marriage to further strengthen the relationship.

Couples may consider seeking financial counseling before marriage as well. Many couples can be reluctant to talk about money or worse, think that the money problems will solve themselves once the marriage starts.

Issues such as debt, poor credit, spending habits (both extreme frugality and frivolous spending) are just some of the many items that should be discussed before entering marriage. They are also good discussion points if they are occurring during marriage.

As you may know, one of the biggest stressors on marriage is finances. By getting financial matters out in the open, discussed earlier on can help both partners understand how they tick financially. This may lead to a better, smoother relationship both emotionally and financially.

Some individuals need to be prepared for some difficult conversations, and potentially, the relationship to end. However, it may be better for the relationship to end before marriage, then to deal with the emotional and financial fallout from divorce.

Couples that are currently married may also consider financial counseling. This is especially important if there are disagreements that cannot be resolved, or if the couple (one or both) feels resentment starting to build.

And if there's nothing wrong? Consider going anyway. Why? It's no different than maintaining your car, house, etc. Nothing may be wrong, but we still maintain and take care of the things that are important to us. Finances in marriage should be no different.

There are several books designed to help couples in need. Also, talking to a qualified professional may be beneficial (not a product pusher). Couples may not know what questions to ask, but a professional may pose questions not thought of, designed to open the lines of communication between a couple.

The Joy of Separate Accounts

As an advisor, I sometimes need to play marriage counselor. Money differences are one of the biggest sources of marital discord. Recently, I resolved a key disagreement that divided a couple. The answer: Let each spouse have his and her own bank account.

The couple – let's call them John and Jane Bickerson – is nearing retirement, and sat down with me to look at their cash flow needs, possible dates to quit working, and the ever-present question, "Do we have enough?"

Frequently, I work with couples who have a hard time agreeing on how much they can spend in retirement, how much they can afford to save, and where to prioritize and allocate the money (to retirement, a wedding, college, etc.).

This couple, however, was different.

The Bickersons had a comfortable net worth, with little, if any, need to worry about funding retirement. But the tension between John and Jane was enormous, and tough to listen to. Jane snipped at John, and John interrupted when Jane talked. These were small jabs, really, and nothing to get too excited about – on the surface. But such disagreements can lead to trouble when people no longer have jobs to fill up their days.

Did they argue about needing more, where to save, who will work longer before retiring? Not at all. They argued about spending on the little things. John was upset because Jane spent money on a local community newspaper subscription. Jane disliked John's buying rare stamps for his collection.

After about 20 minutes of quasi-hostile bantering back and forth, they asked my opinion. I started with a one-word answer: "Autonomy."

I proposed that they each allocate a portion of their earnings each month to separate personal checking accounts. I also suggested that the couple limit their dealings with the other's account to the amount going into it each month. They needn't discuss the purchases they make – it is their money to do with what they want, from newspaper subscriptions to stamp purchases.

Did this work? John and Jane seemed to relax in their chairs. This couple is brilliant on the big things, but let the little things hamper their progress toward their financial planning goals – and bring acrimony to their marriage. They left the office saying they would give it a try.

For couples I recommend this approach to, the results are extremely favorable. Many couples report a sense of freedom. Some even say they use the money to buy gifts for their spouse, bringing back some of the magic of their dating days. Such gifts are surprises, because the other spouse cannot see the purchases in their mutual account.

Autonomy can be a great tool in financial planning for couples. And sometimes being allowed to have independent control on the little things, makes working together on the big things tolerable, if not enjoyable.

Priorities

We've discussed needs versus wants. Along those lines I'd like to talk about priorities. It's common to hear our friends or family say, "I don't have the time" or "I don't have the money" (of course, *we've* never said these words). And periodically, I'll hear these words uttered by my students (no time to study), generally after a not-so-good exam score.

But what these folks are really saying is "It's not a priority *right now*."

For many of us, it's not about having more time or more money. It's about prioritizing the time and money we have. When we reprioritize what's important to us, it's amazing the things we can accomplish and the money we can save. Here are some tips to prioritize your time and money. In fact, for many people time *is* money.

- Prioritize your savings. This can be done by paying yourself first through automatic payroll deduction to your 401(k) or another employer-sponsored plan. Do the same thing with automatic deposits into your IRA from your bank account.

- Determine needs from wants. This is tough for some folks, but doable. Make a list of everything you spend money on monthly and force yourself to eliminate unnecessary things (wants) from necessary expenditures such as retirement savings, emergency funds, or mortgage payment (needs). One you've made the list, allocate your money accordingly and stick with it.

- Don't procrastinate. This is easier said than done. But I would argue that eliminating certain wants (such as cable TV or your smartphone) can free up more time to do things that "you never have time for" such as going back to school, reading or writing a great book, or spending time with family.

  Another neat trick to get more time I learned in college was to set my alarm 1 minute earlier each day than the day before. By doing do, I was able to free up an extra 30 minutes in my day over a month without shocking my body. Eventually, this led to 60 minutes. Now, I have almost two hours to get work done, exercise, and study before my day starts.

312

- Don't create artificial "needs." Artificial needs include credit card debt, car payments, and other expenses that trap you into making payments you are obligated to make but could have avoided with prior planning.

- Set goals. Write down specific goals you'd like to achieve and give them a timeline for accomplishment. For example, you could set baby steps for retirement amounts. This can be done by coming up with an annual savings goal say, $6,500 into an IRA. Give yourself a year (or tax deadline) to accomplish this goal. From there, you can simply divide $6,500 by 12 to get a monthly amount of $500. Use the $500 as a "mini-goal" and try to free up that money from the needs and wants step mentioned above. Once the money's freed up, put it on autopilot as recommended in the first step.

The Airplane Analogy

Many parents face the decision during their working years to try to fund both retirement and college education. Some can adequately do both while others are forced to do the best they can with what money they can save.

Sometimes parents can get caught up in wanting to save as much as they can for their children's college education and forgo the need to save or save more for retirement.

When this situation presents itself, I like to use the airplane analogy. It goes something like this:

Have you ever flown on an airplane before? If you have you know that once you're scrunched in and belted and the plane makes its way from the gate the flight attendants break radio silence and start with their routine flight instructions. After you're taught where the exit rows are and how to use your floatation device they inevitably change the conversation to cabin pressure.

"Should the aircraft experience a decrease in cabin pressure oxygen masks will fall from the overhead compartments. Grab the mask and fully extend the cord to allow the release of oxygen."

The next words are crucial to your survival.

"Place the mask over your face and tighten the straps on the side. Once your mask is secured then attend to your child or help the person next to you."

Why would they say that? Because if you pass out at 35,000 feet you're of no use to anyone.

A similar comparison can be made for those parents saving for both retirement and college. If the focus is solely or mostly on college savings, there may be little if any money accumulated for retirement. In addition, there are plenty of financial aid opportunities available for college. The options for financial aid in retirement are slim.

I'm not saying don't save for your child's education. It is very important and a priority for many parents. What I am saying is make sure your retirement savings are being added to as well. Otherwise the reward for all that money saved for college may be a degree – and future roommates for the graduate!

The Hot Stove Analogy

We've all been there. Cooking dinner around the stove and mistakenly touch the burner or element with our finger. Instantaneously and instinctively our hand immediately withdraws from the heat and we quickly look to see if we need to run it under cold water or worse, grab the bandages.

Individuals can have a similar instinctive reaction when they are burned by the market. When the market is highly volatile their gut reaction may be to pull their hand away quickly and easing the pain by selling and getting out.

It would seem almost malapropos to keep a hand on the hot stove knowing that doing so will result in further pain and injury. And it would be unthinkable to place the *other* hand on the stove, so both are feeling the heat.

Naturally, no one likes to lose money. When markets go down it is perfectly understandable for individuals to not want to subject themselves to further loss and the pain of seeing account values decline. However, for individuals with long time horizons, it can be perfectly sane to keep their hand on the stove (invested in the market). Perhaps a bold few will have the audacity to put *both* hands on the stove (invest more money when markets are down).

Some individuals may want to consider a lukewarm approach by having multiple burners going yet set to different settings (diversification). This way, when one burner is red hot (say, stocks are plummeting) they can place their hands on a different burner (a different, less-correlated asset such as bonds or REITs) and still stay close to the stove, without getting burned.

Your Employee Benefits Package

Starting a new job can be very overwhelming. Often, new-hires go through a barrage of training, information overload and multiple booklets covering procedures, processes and application. Somewhere in that mix is the benefit package. Here is where you can sign up for important health insurance coverage, retirement savings plans, and other benefits such as life insurance and disability.

In the stress and whirlwind of the onboarding process, sometimes benefits can get pushed to the side, and then after time, forgotten about. Additionally, employees generally must wait a full year to make changes (annual enrollment), unless a qualifying event occurs such as a birth, marriage, or divorce.

Here's a checklist of what you, as a new employee can do to make sure you sign up for these precious benefits and some information on how to move forward. If you've been with your employer for some time, it is still a good idea to review what you have and what you have available.

- Select the appropriate health coverage. Some employers have one carrier that provides coverage with different options from that carrier. Options may include HMO, PPO, or HSA plans. The premiums the employee pays will depend on the deductibles in the respective plans, number of covered individuals, and the different benefits offered.

- Sign up for group life insurance. Generally, this is going to be the cheapest life insurance you can get. There's often little underwriting involved, and employees can get anywhere form 1-5 times (sometimes more) of their annual salary in coverage. Some plans allow for spouse and child coverage as well. This coverage should be in addition to your personal policy. The reason being is the coverage may be forfeited if you lose your job or change employers.

- Start saving into the retirement plan. Whether a 401(k), 403(b), or other plan such as a SIMPLE or 457(b), you should start to defer (save) into these plans as soon as you are eligible. Some employers will match your contributions up to a certain amount. *This is free money — never leave it on the table.*

  Additionally, you should consider saving a percent of your income versus a fixed dollar amount. As you receive raises, so too does your contribution increase. This isn't the case with a fixed dollar amount.

- Sign up for short and long-term disability. This covers your income (up to a certain percentage such as 60%) if you become disabled and cannot work for a short or long duration. Premiums are very affordable since it is group coverage and the definition of disability is generally much more favorable than that of Social Security (any occupation).

- Consider other benefits. These other benefits could be discounts on health club memberships, flexible spending accounts (FSAs), employee discounts, etc. Flexible spending accounts (FSAs) allow you to use pre-tax dollars to fund an account that may be used to help pay for certain expenses such as medical and dental expenses and child care expenses.

These are just a few things to consider when becoming a new employee or if you've been at your job for a while. As always, questions can be directed to the employee's HR department or a competent financial professional.

Why You Should Review Beneficiaries

At some point in your life you probably started a new job, applied for life insurance, started a retirement account, or opened a bank account. Remember the forms asked you to name a beneficiary, both primary and contingent, telling the account custodian to whom your account passed if you died? Time's passed and those names you scribbled now loom large in your estate plans.

Your primary beneficiary is the first person who receives your account balance or death benefit. The contingent beneficiary receives the account balance if your primary dies before you. (Some types of accounts also allow you to name a third or tertiary beneficiary.)

Many accounts and financial instruments ask you for beneficiaries: life insurance; retirement plans; U.S. savings bonds; savings accounts, and certificates of deposit; and stocks, bonds and mutual funds (via a Transfer on Death designation), to name a few.

When naming beneficiaries, you picked whether to allocate a portion of the balance or benefit to the primary and the contingent. Possibly you also named two or more primary beneficiaries to each receive a percentage of your account (totaling 100%).

Life changes incessantly. Friends and relatives die, move away, or just lose touch. You forgot about the whole beneficiary thing – until now.

Review and, if necessary, update now your beneficiary designations on your individual retirement accounts, 401(k)s, 403(b) if you work or worked for a school and tax-exempt organization, life insurance, and other savings and brokerage accounts. This becomes especially important if you recently divorced or your primary beneficiary died.

For example, after a couple's nasty divorce, many years pass and both remarry. If neither update beneficiary designations on accounts and policies, guess who gets the proceeds? The ex-spouse.

You may think that having a will means foregoing the naming of beneficiaries and that your will mandates your wishes. Maybe, maybe not. Also, not only is proving your will's validity (called probate) made public record but family members can contest the document – and your last wishes.

For example, let's say a couple's families disagree with the relationship. The families can legally challenge the will of either partner – especially any directives allocating money to the surviving partner.

The couple naming each other as beneficiaries on life insurance and retirement accounts virtually eliminates such a mess. Now operation of contract passes one partner's money to the surviving partner – and avoids the publicity of probate.

Being a beneficiary can bring responsibility; so can naming one. If you name your favorite child as a sole beneficiary and intend for that child to distribute the money equally among all your children, that beneficiary child can in fact *keep all the money* legally.

When considering your beneficiaries, ask yourself some key questions. Do your children or grandchildren need college money or cash to start out in adult life? Do your parents need money for medical bills? Do you have a favorite charity?

Reviewing and updating your beneficiaries only takes a few minutes – a short time that can save you (and your desired beneficiaries) hours, if not years of hassle, hurt, and financial hardship.

Saving for College

If you're a parent or plan to be one, chances are you are considering ways to pay for your child's college education. You may have a goal of sending them to public or private school, with the hope of helping them graduate college with little, if any debt.

Whether or not your goal is to fully fund your child's education or to help as best you can, there are some options to consider saving as much as you can to reach your education savings goal.

One option to consider is a 529 college savings plan. 529 plans allow money to be contributed specifically for many of the costs of higher education. Money that goes into the account grows tax-deferred, and money withdrawn for qualified college education expenses (tuition, room & board, books, fees) is tax-free.

Many states sponsor their own college savings plans, and some allow a state tax deduction for contributions. Currently, there are no federal tax deductions allowed for 529 contributions. 529 plans also have no income limits – meaning that regardless of income, anyone can contribute to a 529 plan.

Additionally, 529 plans have very high lifetime contribution limits ranging from about $300,000 to $400,000 in total, depending on the state plan.

However, the maximum annual contribution limit is $15,000 which is the annual gift tax exclusion. This amount is $30,000 for couples who file jointly. States may also limit the amount of your state tax deduction on contributions.

There is an exception to the annual limit rule which is exclusive to 529 plans. Individuals can make a 5-year pro rata contribution totaling $75,000 (the $15,000 per year exemption multiplied by 5). For married couples filing jointly, the amount is $150,000 (the $30,000 per year exemption multiplied by 5). These numbers are for 2023 and are usually increased annually.

529 plans allow only one beneficiary per 529 plan. The beneficiary may be changed at any time. For example, parents with two children may own one 529 plan with the oldest child named as beneficiary, and then simply change beneficiaries to the younger child when the oldest graduates. Parent can also own one 529 plan for each child. If you're not a parent yet but want to get started, you can open a 529 plan, name yourself beneficiary, and then simply change the beneficiary to your child when he or she is born.

The money in your 529 plan can be invested according to your risk tolerance or timeline. Many plans have predetermined portfolios of stock and bond mutual funds based on your child's age, or they allow you to choose your own allocation based on the funds available.

If the money in a 529 plan is used for non-qualified education expenses the earnings become taxable at your ordinary income tax rates and are also subject to a 10% penalty. States may also recapture any tax deductions taken on contributions.

Exceptions to the 10% penalty include if the beneficiary dies, becomes disabled, or receives a scholarship. It's important to note that in these exceptions, only the 10% penalty is waived. The earnings are still taxable when withdrawn.

Finally, when the time comes to apply for financial aid (grants or student loans) you will likely find yourself filling out the Free Application for Federal Student Aid (FAFSA®). This form essentially determines how much you can contribute toward the costs of college by determining your expected family contribution. 529 plans are considered an asset of the parent (assuming the parent owns it) and the percentage for inclusion in the expected family contribution is much less than assets owned by your child. Non-parent owners of 529 plans, examples of assets owned by children, and other unique circumstances are beyond the scope of this book.

Note: As of 2023 and the passing of the SECURE Act, 529 owners are now allowed to withdraw up to $10,000 to pay for student loans/interest for the beneficiary. Each sibling of the beneficiary is also allowed up to $10,000 for the same expenses.

Does It Really Cost More to Eat Healthy?

From time to time I will hear the argument that it's expensive to eat healthy to lose weight or maintain a healthy lifestyle. What I want to do is provide some information based on my own experience that may help give a counter argument to this belief.

While I am not disagreeing entirely that eating healthy is more expensive than not, I am saying that if done carefully, it is possible to eat healthy for less than what it would cost for less heathy alternatives.

One of the arguments I hear is that individuals may be overweight due to relying on fast food menu items – especially those on dollar or value menus. And the reason these menus are relied on is because shopping for a healthy alternative is pricier.

Let's take a look.

Consider a few value menu items from a well-known fast food provider.

Cheeseburger - $1 – 300 calories.
Small fries - $1 – 230 calories.
Small soft drink - $1 – 150 calories.

Total cost for the meal is $3. Total calories are 680.

This may be a bit extreme, but I am going to calculate this for three meals per day, for 7 days a week. This totals to $9 per day, or $63 for the week. Total calories are 2,040 for the day, or 14,280 for the week. Remember, this is off the dollar menu. Dine-in restaurants are likely much pricier.

In comparison, the local grocery store sells whole grain tortilla wraps for $4.96 a package, containing 16 wraps. This amounts to $0.31 per wrap.

One dozen eggs is about $1.99 or roughly $0.17 per egg (full disclosure: I have my own chickens, so I don't pay for my eggs).

Simply cook two eggs, season with salt and pepper and put in the wrap. Voila!

Assuming this meal was eaten every meal, every day for a week (boring and dull, but doable) this amounts to:

Wrap - $0.31 – 100 calories.
2 eggs - $0.34 – 160 calories.
Glass of water - Free – 0 calories.

The total for each meal is $0.65, or $1.95 daily. This is $13.65 weekly. Total daily calories are 780, which is 5,460 weekly.

Some readers may need to eat more, so doubling this (six small meals per day) would be 1,560 daily and 10,920 weekly calories respectively. If more is needed, simply have two wraps and four eggs (my usual breakfast).

At three meals per day, this is a weekly savings of just over $49. At six meals, it's just over $35 saved.

Am I arguing that one should live just on wraps and eggs alone? No. The point is that with some planning and education, it can be possible to eat healthy, for less than what an unhealthy alternative would be.

Substitutions can be made for the wrap such as whole grain bread ($1.75 a loaf), lettuce ($1.99 for a pound bag) and other substitutes for the egg such as chicken, beef, venison, etc.

Don't be afraid to experiment on your own and see what you can come up with!

Decluttering

Throughout our lives we acquire things. This can start at an early age when we were given things as gifts and of course, the childhood tendency to collect and save many of the items that we came across.

As we mature into adults, the desire or habit to continue to hold onto things may still linger. This leads to garages, basements, closets, bedrooms, and even storage facilities full of stuff. It can also creep into our financial lives – as we acquire different savings accounts, retirement accounts, or purchase things that continue to be automatically deducted from our bank account (a monthly subscription to a gym, perhaps).

Decluttering can have a profound effect on our behavior. It can help lower the stress of trying to keep track of so many things. It can also free up time to enjoy the things in life that are important to us. Finally, it can make a big difference financially when we focus on things we need and allocate our money to priorities that will benefit ourselves and others. Here are some ideas that may help should you decide that decluttering may be beneficial.

- Ask yourself, how often you use/enjoy your stuff. A good rule of thumb is that if it hasn't been used in six months to one year – get rid of it. This includes items such as clothing, kitchenware, clothes, toys, etc. Of course, there will be some exceptions such as holidays decorations, etc., but those items can add up as well.

- Ask yourself if it's a need or a want. Asking this question can help you focus on whether it's necessary, or if you could realistically do without. This may help when contemplating getting rid of monthly subscriptions or infrequently used items such as cable TV, gym memberships, magazine/newspaper subscriptions, etc.

- Could someone else benefit more from the items? This past winter I looked in my closet and saw that I had five different jackets, of which I only wore two. Talk about a first world problem! Some jackets, along with other items not needed anymore, were donated to charity.

- Consolidate accounts. During our lives we have different jobs, get married, divorced, etc. This can lead to having multiple retirement, savings, credit cards, and other accounts. If possible, consolidate those accounts into as few as possible. This will allow you to focus on fewer accounts, and more easily manage your money since it's in fewer places.

- Go paperless. This eliminates the clutter of paper statements filling up your file cabinets and attics. If you can, try to get online billing for bills and make your savings and investing automatic – through bank draft or paycheck deductions to your retirement. Think of this rhetorical question: How many people would save for Social Security if they had to physically write a check?

- Donate your items, don't try to sell them. Except in very rare cases, trying to sell your stuff will only lead to hanging onto it longer – and creating more of a mess and clutter. And while you're at it, skip the garage sale (both having and going to). From an economic standpoint, you're much more financially better off if you donate your stuff and take the tax deduction. I've seen individuals put in over 30 hours of time setting up, monitoring, and working a garage sale to make only $100 or so. And in most cases, most stuff doesn't sell, and it's donated anyway or worse, goes back into storage. What's your time worth?

- Delay gratification. Much clutter and build-up of items we don't use can be attributed to impulse buying. Avoid the temptation to buy on impulse. Infomercials, advertisements, and our peers are constantly bombarding us with the urge to buy more stuff. Take a few moments to gather your thoughts and ask if you really need the item you're about to purchase. Is your money best utilized elsewhere (saving for retirement, college, emergencies, charity)? Paying yourself first helps delay gratification. By paying yourself first and making your retirement and other financial goals priorities, it leaves less money (and temptation) to spend on clutter.

The Power of Compounding

Many individuals understand the power of compound interest. They understand that compound interest means money or interest earned on interest received. That is, if I earn 5 percent interest annually on one dollar, in one year I'll have $1.05, but in two years, I'll have $1.1025, not $1.10.

Granted, this may not seem like a lot; and it isn't. But on several thousand or hundred thousand dollars it really starts to add up. This is mainly for those individuals who haven't heard of this concept or haven't started utilizing it to their advantage. Mainly, I'm addressing millennials and college students.

Those individuals in the cohort I'm addressing have one powerful thing on their side: time. We've discussed the power of time and starting to save early. We showed the comparing of someone starting right away either during or right after college and another start 20 years after college – perhaps in their 40s.

We showed that the individual that started early, ended up having to save *less*, but earned *more* in the long run as compared to the late starter – due to staring early and the power of compounding.

So if you're in college or consider yourself a millennial, consider starting to save today in an IRA, your employer's 401(k), or a non-qualified investment account. Additionally, there's also another way to take advantage of compounding – and that is continuing to invest in your human capital.

Investing in your human capital means continuing education such as a designation, advanced degree, or personal development through reading books or taking courses in an area of study. This compounding of knowledge can help boost your income which will then allow you to save more and have more both now and for retirement.

To get started, consider exploring your employer's plan. Try to save at least 15 percent of your gross income and aim for 20 percent or higher. The sooner you start and the higher percentage you choose the better. You won't miss it. From there, consider opening and contributing to an IRA. In addition, explore options that may increase your human capital such as a master's degree, PhD or other coursework.

However, carefully consider if the expense of such a degree or coursework will compound for you. What

I mean is it's important to analyze whether the advanced degree makes sense financially. If the advanced degree will cost five to six figures, but return very little in regard to financial increase, you may consider another route. While I am in favor of education, the last thing an individual wants to do is wind up six figures in debt without a significant financial return on that investment.

Finally, consider giving of your time and resources to others. Your generosity and advice to others compounds in ways you may not see physically (such as monetary or other rewards) but it will reward you holistically and potentially spiritually. After all, is anyone self-made? I would argue no. They had help from others along their journey – both seen and unseen. And with some luck as well, they were able to make the most of what they were given - so will you; and it will continue to compound.

Create Your Own Luck

"Luck is when preparation meets opportunity."

The other day I was eating lunch with my kids. After lunch was over I gave them a "treat" from the drawer that we normally house goodies of all sorts. I happened to grab a couple of gold-wrapped chocolate coins. These coins were renditions of the JFK half-dollars. My youngest grabbed her coin and said, "heads or tails?" I quickly said "heads" while she flipped the coin in the air.

The coin landed on the floor – showing tails. I said, "Well, we both lost." My daughter quickly exclaimed, "I won daddy." When I asked her how she won when the coin landed tails she replied to me, "I called both heads and tails."

Win-win.

Essentially, my daughter had created her own luck. And I immediately thought, "This is excellent fodder to write about. So here we are.

The reason why I mention this is to raise the rhetorical question of how do we create our own luck? As the quote at the beginning of the post mentions, I believe luck is when preparation meets opportunity. In other words, it's possible to create our own luck.

So how do we prepare to meet opportunity? From a financial planning perspective, there are many ways. Of course, these can be applied to many other facets of life – not just financial.

One way is to create an emergency fund. With a properly funded emergency fund, when an emergency arises, we will have the financial resources to cover the ordeal. In other words, the preparation meets the opportunity. And we're lucky to have had the money to cover it.

Another way is to save as much as we can for retirement. In preparing for 20, 30, or more years in retirement by saving now, when the opportunity to retire comes, we are prepared to meet it. Again, we are "lucky" to have a stable, financially rewarding retirement.

More examples include continuing to learn and educate ourselves (in preparation for the opportunity for career advancement, income increases, passing our knowledge to others), as well as why we carry auto, home, life, disability, and other insurances (in the event of an unlucky situation, we are lucky to have the insurance to cover it).

I hope you see the point.

Finally, don't be afraid to look for luck. I consider myself pretty good at finding four-leaf clovers. Many times, people have asked me how I am able to find so many. My reply is that I *look* for them. Seek opportunities to be lucky.

Later that same day my kids asked if they could get a dog. I said that now is not the right time. I mentioned all the responsibility that comes with a pet – training, feeding, walking, etc.

My daughters explained that they had done some "research" and found that puppies can be house trained using training pads, and cats can be trained to a litter box. And if we didn't like the smell, we could put the box in the garage. If we were worried about shedding, we could get a dog that doesn't shed.

Clearly, they had done their homework – they had prepared. They were creating their own luck.

My goal is to make the opportunity less available...***wish me luck!***

Perspective

Let's think about perspective. In other words, how do we look at things? How do we see the world? Perspective is important when it comes to our lives and finances.

Here are few examples to ponder:

- A millionaire does his or her best to legally reduce their tax bill and some would say that they are making too much money and should pay much more in taxes. Looking at it differently, the millionaire gave several hundred thousand dollars away to charity (some see it as reducing their tax bill) but they are a philanthropist who funds education, vaccines, and other noble causes.

- A person investing in the market watches it crash and liquidates their entire portfolio. Another investor sees this as the market trading at fire-sale prices and buys as much as they can – buying low, often from the investor selling low to liquidate.

- A husband says that he doesn't want or need life insurance because he doesn't want his wife to be rich when he dies. Another husband buys as much as he can, so his wife is financially secure if he dies.

These examples reflect the glass half-full/half-empty mentality. How we feel and respond to things is a direct reflection of how we perceive them. Sometimes we need to look at things differently to change our perspective. By looking at things differently, we open the doors for opportunity and can minimize loss.

Here's a personal example. I love to garden. Some years ago, I had planted a raspberry patch. Over time the canes spouted growth and started to throw off blossoms. For a period of about two weeks, I didn't check on them and went out one day to see if there were any berries. To my dismay, there was gorgeous, lush green foliage but no sign of berries. I was disappointed. Dejected, I started walking away when something stopped me, and I felt compelled to go back to the patch but look at it differently.

As silly as it was, I got down on my hands and knees and then laid on my back. I scooted under the leaves like a mechanic about to change oil in a car. My neighbors must have thought it was funny seeing only a lush green berry patch and feet sticking out!

When I looked up all I saw was red!

Berries everywhere!

By changing how I looked at things I went from dismay to over 3 gallons of berries. Imagine if I wouldn't have looked. All those wasted berries.

What are you wasting, missing out on, and losing by not changing your perspective?

Without Action, Nothing Happens

Every New Year it seems almost cliché to talk about resolutions or goals. Although making resolutions and goals is not a bad thing, I thought I'd spend some time talking about an arguably more important aspect to resolutions and goals; and that is taking action.

To help make some sense with this I thought I'd share a personal experience. When I was in college I was considerably overweight. Between my junior and senior year, I lost quite a bit of weight – about 75 pounds. I was never overweight growing up; I had just let poor eating habits and a sedentary lifestyle get the best of me.

After the weight came off, friends and family asked me what I did and what my secret was. Really, there was no secret. It was simply eating less and exercising more. However, I became infatuated with diet and exercise and began to research and study more about how to live a healthier lifestyle.

As I put what I was learning into my own practice, friends and family began to ask me if I would put what I learned together in an easy-to-follow format (a written plan if you will) so that they could follow the program and hopefully obtain similar results.

Unfortunately, some that wanted help lost their enthusiasm, stopped following their plan, and gave up. Then, at certain times of the year (say, when making another New Year's resolution) they would come back and ask me to write a new plan for them, so they could get back on track and live a healthier lifestyle.

My answer, to their surprise, was no.

The reason why wasn't to be rude or unaccommodating. It was the fact that *nothing had changed*. In other words, the plan I had given them previously was just as effective and would help them live a healthier lifestyle. The problem was whether they would act and utilize the information in the plan.

The same is true for many other goals and resolutions including the personal finance topics covered in this book. The best financial plan in the world is completely useless unless action is taken to implement the steps in the plan.

A resolution to save for retirement is meaningless unless action is taken to physically have the money from your paycheck invested in your 401(k), IRA, or other retirement plan. Resolving to pay off debt without taking action to pay down the debt is useless. You get the point.

Although this book presents several financial topics from which you may create goals, I think it's equally important to write about taking these same goals, maybe some from this year and years past, and *acting* on them. This year, instead of making a repeat list of financial resolutions, make a list of action steps you're going to take to make those goals a reality.

Good luck!

And thank you!

Appendix

This book was originally written in 2019, and many of the numbers may change (such as retirement plan contribution limits) as time passes and new laws are introduced.

The following are links resources that you can read from time to time to stay current with laws, regulations, and most importantly – your plan.

Of course, should you work with a fiduciary advisor, he or she should be up-to-date in many of these areas as well.

Disclosure: I receive no financial compensation from any of the following entities.

Retirement Plans

https://www.irs.gov/retirement-plans/plan-sponsor/types-of-retirement-plans

https://www.pbgc.gov/ (Pension benefit Guaranty Corporation)

College Savings and Tax Benefits

https://www.irs.gov/publications/p970

Taxation

https://www.irs.gov/individuals

https://www.irs.gov/filing (Tax forms and filing information)

https://www.irs.gov/businesses/small-businesses-self-employed/estate-and-gift-taxes (Information on estate and gift taxation)

Investing

https://investor.vanguard.com/corporate-portal/ (The leading provider of low-cost index funds)

https://www.fidelity.com/ (Another source for index funds)

https://www.tdameritrade.com/home.page (Brokerage company with access to thousands of securities)

https://www.morningstar.com/ (Research ratings, fees, expenses, on ETFs, mutual funds, stocks, and bonds)

https://us.spindices.com/spiva/#/reports
(Research showing how active fund managers perform compared to their benchmark (index))

Professional Advice

https://adviserinfo.sec.gov/ (Background check for advisors/fiduciaries)

https://brokercheck.finra.org/ (Background check for brokers, registered representatives)

https://www.cfp.net/ (Find and research CFP® professionals)

Social Security

https://www.ssa.gov/

www.ingramcontent.com/pod-product-compliance
Lightning Source LLC
Chambersburg PA
CBHW021349210526
45463CB00001B/34